THE MARTYR
Bhagat Singh—Experiments in Revolution

THE MARTYR
Bhagat Singh—Experiments in Revolution

KULDIP NAYAR

HAR-ANAND
PUBLICATIONS PVT LTD

HAR-ANAND PUBLICATIONS PVT LTD
D-9, Anand Niketan, New Delhi - 110 021
Tel. 4101983, 4101962 Fax : 011-5124868
E-mail: haranand@mantraonline.com
Website:www.har-anandpublications.com

Sole Distributors of Paper Backs
Diamond Pocket Books Pvt. Ltd.
X-30, Okhla Industrial Area, Phase-II, New Delhi-110020 (India)
Phones: (Off.) 6822803, 6822804, 6841033
Facsimile: +91 (011) 6925020
email: mverma@nde.vsnl.net.in

PRINTED IN INDIA

Published by Ashok Gosain and Ashish Gosain for Har-Anand Publications Pvt Ltd and printed at H.S. Offset Printers.

This book is dedicated
to my grand-children,
Mandira, Kartik and Kanika

Preface

There is no arch, no plaque, not even a stone in Pakistan to commemorate the execution of Bhagat Singh and his two comrades, Sukhdev and Rajguru. Lahore Central jail, where the three revolutionaries were hanged on 23 March, 1931, has been mostly demolished. Their cells have been razed to the ground as if the establishment did not want any sign of their execution to remain.

Ironically, the authorities have allowed a colony, Shadman (abode of happiness), to come up at the site. Minarets of an elegant mosque rise right opposite the place where Bhagat Singh's cell stood before the demolition. The road between the mosque and the remaining part of the jail ends at the entrance of a mental hospital.

I asked residents of Shadman if they knew who Bhagat Singh was. Many of them had heard his name. Some had a vague idea of his confinement and hanging. "When we came here, there were only police quarters, which were pulled down as the colony expanded," said a man in his fifties.

The scaffold, where the three were hanged, has been turned into a traffic roundabout. Vehicles ply there as waywardly as in the rest of Lahore. Noise, smoke and dust shroud the crossing.

There is a story about the roundabout which has been told and retold after the execution of former Prime Minister Zulfikar Ali Bhutto more than two decades ago. This is the place where Nawaz Mohammad Ahmed Khan, father of Ahmed Raza Kasuri, then a member of Pakistan's National Assembly, was shot at. Bhutto had reportedly ordered the killing of Kasuri. When the bullets were fired through automatic weapons, Kasuri was negotiating the roundabout. His father, sitting next to him, received fatal injuries at the very spot where the scaffold stood. Kasuri's grandfather was one of the officials who had identified the bodies of the three revolutionaries. Old timers believe that nemesis caught up with the Kasuri family when Mohammad Ahmed Khan was wounded at the roundabout. The story made a deep impression on me and I thought I would write about Bhagat Singh one day.

The idea of a book matured subsequently in Lahore itself. The city was the venue of the World Punjabi Conference in the eighties. The hall where the conference was held had only one photograph, that of Bhagat Singh. I asked the organisers why they had ignored a distinguished Punjabi on their side, Mohammad Iqbal, the renowned Urdu poet who visualised the concept of Pakistan. Their reply was that there was only one Punjabi who sacrificed his life for the country's independence and his name was Bhagat Singh.

Still the thought of a book on Bhagat Singh remained smouldering within me. I believed that practically everything about him had been written time and again. But then I received a letter from Harjinder Singh and Sukhjinder Singh, who were awaiting a death sentence for assassinating General A.S.Vaidya, former Chief of Army Staff, at Pune. What they wrote prodded me to think about the book seriously. They questioned the basis on which Bhagat Singh was hailed a revolutionary while they were described as terrorists. They said that they too had served a cause: Bhagat Singh had avenged the death of Lajpat Rai, the Lion of Punjab, at the hands of a British police officer while they had settled scores with Vaidya for planning the attack in 1984 on the Golden Temple, their Vatican. Fearing that more and more militants would compare themselves with Bhagat Singh, I thought it would be worthwhile to trace his life and philosophy, and explain the difference between terrorism and revolution.

What did killing mean to a revolutionary? Bhagat Singh explained it in his own words: "We attach great sanctity to human life, we regard man's life as sacred...We would sooner lay down our lives in the service of humanity than injure anyone."

There was no revenge, no vendetta. "These actions (killings)," he said, "have their political significance in as much as they serve to create a mentality and an atmosphere which shall be very necessary to the final struggle. That is all."

I could find time only off and on for research, which began seven years ago. The Archives of Pakistan is possibly the best source. But it is not open to Indians. New Delhi and Islamabad have no agreement which allows nationals of one country access to the archives of the other. I approached the Pakistan government through a friend. A lame excuse was offered to deny me access. They said they were afraid they might get entangled in the Sikh problem. I could not figure out the connection with the 1931 execution except that Bhagat Singh was a Sikh.

The India Office Library in London has practically nothing on him. In any case, the library has distributed most of its books, reports and documents all over the UK. This is meant to stop India, Pakistan and Bangladesh, ex-colonies of Great Britain, from ever staking their claim to what should have come to them after independence. After the Partition of the subcontinent, India and Pakistan could not agree upon a formula for the division of the library, thus giving the UK a pretext to gobble it up entirely.

Some information on an appeal in the Privy Council against the death sentences on the three revolutionaries is available. This is in our archives as well. My feeling is that crucial files have been destroyed or kept back. Secret telegrams or papers must be somewhere to show that the British establishment was determined to hang Bhagat Singh and his two comrades to smother the revolutionary ferment. The ideas had taken root in India from the French Revolution, the American Declaration of Independence, and the Bolshevik Revolution in Russia. The struggle against social evils, the awakening of oppressed castes and the rise of peasants and workers against social oppression and inequalities all became an integral part of the freedom struggle.

In the midst of my research, I found that Bhagat Singh wrote as many as four books in jail. *The History of the Revolutionary Movement in India*, *The Ideal of Socialism*, *Autobiography* and *At The Door of Death*. I vainly tried to locate them. I was told that the manuscripts, which were smuggled out of jail before the execution and kept by the revolutionaries in custody, were handed over in the forties to Kumari Lajyavati, who later became the principal of Kendriya Mahavidyalaya, Jalandhar. Lajyavati, who is now dead, reportedly gave them to someone in Lahore just before Partition to send to India. This someone, not identified, is said to have told her that he burnt all the manuscripts in panic before migrating to India in August, 1947. The story is not credible. I still think that the manuscripts will appear one day.

The first thing I did while collecting material for the book was locate Bhagat Singh's two brothers. Kultar Singh, the younger one, was in Sharanpur. His information about Bhagat Singh's last meeting with close relatives was useful. I found that the family had a nationalistic streak running through it. Bhagat Singh's uncle, Ajit

Singh, shared a prison cell with Lajpat Rai in Burma when Bhagat Singh was born. His grandfather openly contributed to the Congress party. I also got in touch with Kulbir Singh, the older brother. But he died before we could meet.

In December 1992, I was able to trace Mathura Das Thapar, Sukhdev's younger brother. I wrote him a letter that very month. Thapar replied to me in March 1993. His tale of woe was touching. He said he had to leave Lyallpur (renamed Faislabad by Pakistan) "due to the constant troubles created against me by the Punjab Police on account of my being the blood brother of Sukhdev".

Thapar, then 82, was bitter. In his reply to my letter, he said: "Allow me the indulgence to add that the other political sufferers like Dr. Kichlew's son, got a monthly packet of Rs. 5,000 and a flat, free of cost. Against Dr. Kichlew's son, compare our clan's sacrifice." He drew my attention to the 'Proceedings Book of the Lahore Conspiracy Case' which he had brought from Pakistan and had deposited with the National Archives in New Delhi. These proceedings have marginal comments by Sukhdev, who was able to read them before the execution. Pakistan has the original proceedings in Urdu which I have gone though.

Thapar's letter, which I retain (See Annexure 1), ended with the remark: "Hoping to be of use in your great task of writing the masterpiece of great historical importance." He died before we could meet. I do not know how he would have assessed this book. My work may not be 'a masterpiece'. But I have tried my best to present Bhagat Singh as he lived, thought and died.

In a family's collection, I read the correspondence between Thapar and Hans Raj Vohra, who had turned approver. The correspondence, particularly Vohra's letter explaining his decision so, and Thapar's comments form the epilogue of my book.

Through Kultar Singh, I learnt that Durga Devi, wife of Bhagwati Charan, a leading revolutionary of those days, lived in Ghaziabad with her son. Although she suffered frequent memory lapses, when I met her four years ago, she was able to reconstruct the story of Bhagat Singh's escape from Lahore after the assassination of Deputy Superintendent of Police J.P. Saunders. She died a few months ago.

Several books on Bhagat Singh and his own writings have helped me narrate the story and philosophy of his life. Words attributed to him have been culled from his letters, statements or speeches. I have not taken any liberties with the facts.

The police records of those days gave me an insight into the methods used by the British to suppress the revolutionaries. Intelligence reports, very few in our archives, have also been of some assistance. A repository of information is a six-volume collection of documents *Terrorism in Bengal* during the British period brought out by the Government of West Bengal. I have made use of some information from the collection.

Many of Mahatama Gandhi's writings throw light on his attitude towards the revolutionaries. He admired their courage but not their use of guns and bombs. He did not doubt their commitment but he was definite that force could not release India from the clutches of British power. Gandhi and Bhagat Singh were diametrically opposed to each other in approach. Bhagat Singh believed in violence and did not flinch from using it to achieve independence. Gandhi, on the other hand, remained wedded to non-violence all his life and brooked no other approach. They represented two different strands of the struggle for India's independence.

It was a tribute to Bhagat Singh when Pattabhi Sitaramayya, who wrote the history of the Congress, said that Gandhi and Bhagat Singh mere equally popular, the first because of his experiments with truth and the second because of his essays in bravery. Bhagat Singh was 21 when he saw Gandhi for the first time. The Mahatma was then 59.

I have gone through newspapers of those days. I have also talked to people, who have knowledge about Bhagat Singh. There are not many left. The best source was a friend, Virendra, editor of *The Pratap*, Jalandhar. He died five years ago. He was in Lahore Central Jail when the trial of Bhagat and his comrades was going on. Virendra too was a suspect. But nothing credible was found against him. He was released after a stint in prison.

Many people have helped me complete the book. They include Kavita, my younger daughter-in-law, who researched the trial; and R. Ramachandaran, Subramanyam and Gopal, who typed and retyped the draft before keying it into a computer. I thank them all. I am also grateful to Neelima Rao, who has designed the book's cover.

Contents

One

He recognised the footsteps. Head Jail Warden Charat Singh was shuffling along feebly. A stint in the army and a long service with the police had affected his health. His white beard made him look older than his age.

Handcuffed and shackled, Bhagat Singh could sense his approach. Sentenced to death by a British Tribunal nearly six months ago on October 7, 1930, he was still waiting behind the high walls of Lahore Central Jail for the hanging. He had seen daylight creeping into his cell No. 14, lingering and receding in the twilight of the evening. He had listened to the sound of silence endlessly, interrupted by the hourly sound of a jail gong and the clang of an iron door, whenever it was opened or closed.

When the sun was down, the darkness was really thick, with no electric bulb, no lantern, not even an earthen lamp to light his cell. Somewhere, in the distance, a searchlight revolved to provide a semblance of illumination to the area where he, along with his two comrades, Sukhdev and Rajguru, awaited the hanging. The cell was a dungeon with grass on the floor and a smelly hole in a corner.

When Bhagat Singh stretched himself, there was just enough space to accommodate his 5 feet and 10 inch body. But he had become used to this harsh, drab life. He had felt autumn changing into winter when a tattered blanket was thrown at him to fight the below three degree centigrade temperatures. The advent of March had lessened the rigour. There was a promise of spring in the air. But the very name given to the cell, Phansi ki Kothi (The Hanging Cell), blighted any pleasant thoughts. Circumscribed in space and time, he could not see the change in weather.

Bhagat Singh had learnt to live in solitude. Yet he was impatient, not because he was isolated but because it had been a long and purposeless wait. He sometimes wished they would carry out the execution quickly. But then he felt his life of 23 years had been too short. He once wrote to a friend that he had not accomplished even a thousandth of what he had proposed to do.

He later told a comrade, Vijay Kumar Sinha, who met him a fortnight before the execution, "It would be a calamity if I am spared. If I die, wreathed in smiles, India's mothers would wish their children to emulate Bhagat Singh and thus, the number of formidable freedom fighters would increase so much that it would be impossible for the satanic powers to stop the march of revolution."

Bhagat Singh was perceptive enough to realise that their execution had got linked with political developments in the country. The British had drawn a blank on the Round Table Conference that they called in London in November 1930. They wanted to ladle out limited powers for 'self-governance' but found no takers. India was then seething with discontent. The Congress party, which led the national struggle for independence, had boycotted the conference. Other parties also followed the Congress.

Bhagat Singh was not opposed to compromise. He believed it was not such a deplorable thing but was an indispensable factor in political strategy. Any nation that rose against its oppressors was bound to fail in the beginning but would later gain partial reforms through compromises.

The Russian Revolution, which inspired India's revolutionaries, was one example. After the 1917 revolution, when the Bolsheviks were forced to sign the Brest Litovsk Treaty, everybody except Lenin was opposed to it. He said: "Peace and again peace: peace at any cost—even at the cost of many of the Russian provinces to be yielded to German War Lords." When criticised, he admitted that since the Bolsheviks could not face the German onslaught, he had to compromise.

London favoured some agreement through another Round Table Conference. But it did not want the corpse of Bhagat Singh lying between England and India when the talks took place. The British therefore deferred the hanging while they explored all avenues to reach a settlement, primarily with the Congress, or Gandhi who guided the party.

Charat Singh stood outside the cell, fumbling for the right key from the bunch of keys he took out from the long pocket of the fatigues he wore. He and Bhagat Singh had developed a fondness for each other. They talked in Punjabi, their mother tongue.

Life is a strange experience; the shorter it is, the more poignant it is in intensity. Both knew that their contact would snap soon. But it did not stop them from becoming close to each other. Charat

Singh, a deeply religious person, would often advise him to chant the name of Waheguru now that his end was near. Bhagat Singh would reply: "Don't you think it is too late?"

Was the meeting on March 3, an *akhiri mulaqat* (final meeting) with his close relatives, a legal obligation before the hanging? Or would there be another meeting? Bhagat Singh wanted to know so as to prepare himself to say goodbye to his relatives. Charat Singh did not say anything. Bhagat Singh did not insist. He realised the warden's compulsions.

Charat Singh had been kind to him. The warden had allowed Bhagat Singh to smuggle in all the books he wanted to read. It was all Marxist literature, strictly banned by the government. Still that was what he read or literally devoured. Hardly would a book on Marx, Lenin or Russia arrive when he would put in a demand for more. The secret supply by the local Dwarka Dass Library, founded by progressive nationalists, could not keep pace with his speed of reading. So keen was he about books that he once wrote to his schoolmate, Jaidev, to draw from the library, *Militarism* by Karl Liebknecht, *Left-Wing Communism, Why Men Fight* by Bertrand Russell, *Land Revolution in Russia* and *Spy* by Upton Sinclair, and send them to him through Kulbir, his brother.

'Study' was the cry that reverberated through the corridors of Bhagat Singh's mind, study to enable himself to face the arguments advanced by the opposition, study to arm himself with reasons in favour of his cult of revolution and study methods to change the system in India. Indeed, Bhagat Singh's passion since his childhood was books. He taught himself Marxism, communism and revolutionary philosophy. They gave him a different perspective on life.

Coming from a clan of freedom fighters, the urge to participate in the struggle for independence was natural. But his was a landed family. Awakening to socialistic ideas was something new to him. How could political freedom mean anything without economic freedom? What would be the point of freedom if the poor remained poor? And how would the disparities between the rich and the poor go? Books made him realise that social disparities were created by man and perpetuated by man.

He regarded Karl Marx as his guru. The German thinker said that a change in the balance of economic power was the rationale upon which depended all other changes of human history. Political history, the history of thought, of religions and the rest were born in the womb of economic circumstances. Never before had he appreciated Dialectical Materialism—that political theory was not prior, but posterior, to political fact. Marx made him feel that political actions were not the cause; they were the products of economic forces.

The struggle for independence in India was basically a struggle for economic improvement. Freedom would provide an opportunity for improvement. An independent India, without removing poverty, would be free only in name. Bhagat Singh did not want to substitute the status quo with another status quo.

He had once written to his mother: "Ma, I have no doubt that my country will be one day free. But I am afraid that the brown sahibs are going to sit in the chairs the white sahibs will vacate." People's plight would remain the same if it meant only a change of masters. He was convinced that no change was possible without the destruction of the antiquated system. That was what stood like a wall in the way of progress. Philosophers had interpreted the world in different ways. But the real point was to change it. Revolution alone could do so.

He was not alone. There were hundreds of revolutionaries like him. They had come together and reinvigorated the dying Hindustan Republican Association. Bhagat Singh had added the word 'socialist' to its name. Sukhdev and Rajguru, shut in adjoining cells, cherished the same dreams. And so did many others from the United Province (now Uttar Pradesh), Punjab and Rajputana (now part of Rajasthan). They were all there on September 8-9, 1928, at Ferozeshah Kotla in New Delhi where the party was rechristened the Hindustan Socialist Republican Association (HSRA). The Bengal revolutionaries had stayed away from the meeting—and the party— because they had abandoned the use of bombs or revolvers.

The HSRA had also constituted an armed wing and put it under Chandra Shekhar Azad, a senior revolutionary and the best shot in the party. The armed wing was for collecting arms and ammunition and arranging mass action. Then there were sympathisers doing propaganda, raising money and arranging shelter for members of armed wings.

Sukhdev and Rajguru stood behind iron bars as Bhagat Singh passed by them, following the measured steps of Charat Singh. Nobody had come to meet them. Rajguru had told Bhagat Singh that he had no close relatives and expected nobody. Sukhdev said his uncle had promised to come. Apparently, he had not turned up either. Bhagat Singh felt sad. He could not imagine anyone's family members staying away when there was an opportunity—probably the last one—to meet their own blood before death.

The family was Bhagat Singh's refuge. He had spent only a few early years at home. Yet he felt close to his relatives. All of them were there. He was overwhelmed to see his mother although he had written to his father not to bring her along. She did not stop weeping at the last meeting. Deputy Superintendent Khan Bahadur Akbar Khan went on extending the time of their meeting despite contrary instructions from above.

Bhagat Singh found that his grandfather, Arjun Singh—who had given him his name, Bhagat and called him Bhagatu—was unusually sad. His father, Kishen Singh's long white beard was glistening with tears. Kulbir, his younger brother, was wiping his cheeks. Kultar, the youngest, 10 years old, was sobbing. His mother's dupatta was wet. She was trying to push back her tears. The three sisters—Amar Kaur, Sumitra Kaur and Shakuntala Kaur— were on the verge of breaking down.

Bhagat Singh had sent them a message not to bid him a tearful farewell. He wanted his last meeting to be full of happy moments, which he would recall when he walked towards the scaffold. Finding them drowned in sorrow, he got worried. He could understand that they would feel the loss. But they should have known that death was inevitable on the path he had chosen. He implored them to stay together and bear the loss bravely.

He was particularly worried about his mother who, unlike his father, generally kept her grief bottled up inside. It showed on her face, which had wrinkled prematurely. She touched his long hair rolled on the top of his head. She was unhappy when he had cut it off. Caressing him, she said: "Everyone had to die one day. But the best death was the one which the world should cherish." She told him to shout Inquilab Zindabad when he stood at the gallows.

Bhagat Singh could see his mother's eyes fixed on him all the time as if she wanted to treasure every gesture of his. Her grief would be uncontrollable after he was hanged. He could see the tears trickling down from her eyes.

"If you go on crying, Ma, I shall not be able to hold back myself," he said. "I do not want people to say that there were tears even in the eyes of Bhagat Singh's mother when he was hanged. This did not become her or the family of freedom fighters."

Why should she cry? For that matter, why should anybody cry? He had committed no crime. He had taken up arms to drive out foreign rulers from the country. Nobody had any right to enslave others. The British were as unwanted in India as were the French, the Portugese or other powers wherever they ruled. Freedom was indivisible. He wanted not only India but all the enslaved countries in the world to be free.

No nation was good enough to rule another. He was against masters and all those who exploited people. Freedom itself was revolution. Revolution was not the cult of the bomb or the pistol. Nor was it a personal vendetta. It sought to change the order so that the subjugated were free.

His mother brought him back to his place of birth, the childhood he spent in his village, Banga, roaming dusty streets with boys of his age. He remembered how he endlessly argued with his father on every point. Whenever his father took him to task for *baghawati* (revolutionary) work, she would stand by him. She never defied her husband. But she always managed to pacify him. She was the one who would resolve differences between the son and the father. Sometime the two did not speak to each other for days.

Her influence on Bhagat Singh was deep. It was she who persuaded him to return home when he left after his father insisted on his marriage. In a letter to his father, he had argued that his life was committed to India's freedom. "You must be remembering that at the time of my sacred thread ceremony early in years, Papuji (grandfather) had declared that I was being pledged for the service of the country. I am, therefore, honouring the pledge of that time. I hope you will forgive me."

His father never wanted Bhagat Singh to follow him or his uncle, Ajit Singh, who had raised the standard of revolt against the British. Bhagat Singh treasured his uncle's book, *Muhibb-e-Watan* (patriots), which he had personally given him. He had seen the marks left behind by wounds inflicted by the British on his uncle's body.

After his father realised that Bhagat Singh was not a person who could be stopped from participating in revolutionary activities, all that he advised him was to be careful. It was not unnatural for a father to do so. Caution did not mean cowardice. But Bhagat Singh had thrown caution to the wind. Those who wanted the country to be released from British bondage would have to come out in the open and be counted, he believed.

Gandhi was in touch with the viceroy to stop the hanging, his father said. Bhagat Singh had little faith in Gandhi or his non-violence. The British would not quit until forced. Freedom had to be wrested from the hands of rulers. It would not fall from the sky. He had not forgiven Gandhi for the withdrawal of the non-cooperation movement against the rulers some 10 years ago. Every sequence was etched in his mind.

Gandhi gave a call for non-cooperation at a Congress meeting in November 1920. Students renounced their studies, lawyers their practice, doctors their clinics and civil servants their jobs and rallied behind him from all over the country. More than 30,000 people went to jail. Foreign goods were boycotted. Piles of textile were burnt in public to protest against imported cloth from Lancashire and Birmingham. Gandhi had said that love of foreign cloth had brought foreign domination. He wanted the British to "declare in clear terms a policy of absolute non-interference with all non-violent activities in the country". Indeed, non-cooperation was the biggest non-violent movement the Indians had ever launched against the British.

Yet Gandhi withdrew it suddenly. He did not approve of villagers from Chauri Chaura, near Gorakhpur (UP), turning violent. But what was their fault? On February 12, 1921, they took out a procession past a local police station to protest against British rule. Towards the end, the procession was jeered at by the police, provoking the people to retaliate. The policemen, numbering 23, ordered the processionists to disperse. But they stood their ground firmly and peacefully. Angry policemen then started firing on them and went on doing so till their ammunition was exhausted. Three men were killed and many injured. The infuriated crowd set fire to the police station where 21 policemen were either burnt alive or cut into pieces and thrown into the fire. Gandhi withdrew the movement but did not utter a word to condemn the police.

No revolutionary, Bhagat Singh thought, would have done that because such incidents were the essence of uprisings. They had their own logic, their own way of churning politics. Stopping them was like pouring cold water on the fire of defiance which would have spread. All was fair when a country was engaged in a war of liberation.

He felt India lost at that time a great opportunity to bring the enemy to its knees. What was possible that day might not be possible the next day. The loss of a few days, even a single day, postponed not only the deliverance of the people but also defeated the psychological moment. Bhagat Singh could understand why the villagers had retaliated. They had been driven to the wall. They had to hit back. The important point was to get rid of the rulers, not the manner in which it was done.

Bhagat Singh told his father that he could neither understand Gandhi's political strategy, nor his moral approach, which had hacked the movement to pieces with a single blow. Non-violence was all right up to a point. It helped build popular response. But he could not understand or appreciate the strategy or morality of an act which dealt a fatal blow to a popular movement at its peak.

An alien rule could not be defeated through kidgloves, an iron fist was required. At times, it was inevitable. Force when aggressively applied was violence and morally unjustifiable but when it was used for a legitimate cause, it had moral justification.

Bhagat Singh did not agree with Gandhi that right results would not come from wrong methods. It was the goal which mattered. If people recovered their freedom by force, their actions were justified.

Bhagat Singh told his father that Gandhi's non-violence was an excuse for inaction. It was a cover for cowardice. He had no faith in his leadership, or his creed of non-violence. Gandhi was a kind-hearted person. But it was not philanthropy which was required. The British must fear India. He did not want to join issue with his father at the last meeting. However, he conceded that they would be ungrateful if they did not salute the Mahatma for the immense awakening that he had generated through the non-cooperation movement in the country. But the Mahatma was an impossible visionary. The revolutionaries respected him but did not want to follow him. Bhagat Singh found his father relieved when he uttered the word 'respect' for Gandhi.

Revenge was a reality, not a passive vision. Bhagat Singh believed that oppression should evoke feelings of retaliation, not mere protest. Violence was the catharsis for the oppressed. It was a cleansing force. It freed the subjugated from their inferiority complex, their despair. It made them fearless and restored their self-respect. It was a phase, an inevitable phase of the revolution.

Yet he did not favour of terrorism. Killing was senseless; it often targeted the innocent. Acts of terrorism were meant to display power and win publicity. Revolution was an act of defiance, not of violence. It was an ideological war. Terrorism did not go beyond the limits of revenge. It was anger against an individual, not the establishment. It aggravated violence and sidetracked the issue of social transformation. It only instilled fear. True, courage was involved, but not idealism. Terrorism lowered society in its own eyes.

A revolutionary fought for the improvement of the society that oppressed him. He was part of it. At the same time, he tried to transcend it through his efforts for a change. His struggle was against the system, the exploitation of man by man, nation by nation. His sacrifice purged ugliness. Revolutionary change was a qualitative alteration of existing social relations and created new human beings who were superior in moral and material terms.

The cult of martyrdom was what Bhagat Singh liked most in Sikhism, the faith he was born to. He would often recall the words of Gobind Singh, the tenth Sikh Guru. "It is incumbent on people to sacrifice their life to strengthen the cause they uphold." He derived inspiration from the Guru's words: *'Chidiyan noo baaz nall ladaoon, taan Guru Gobind Singh kahalson.'* (Only when I make sparrows fight with eagles, am I called Guru Gobind Singh.)

But Bhagat Singh did not believe in Sikhism or any other religion. He was an atheist. For him religion was a disease, born out of fear. It was opium for the masses. He remembered the words of Marx: "Man makes religion, religion does not make man."

His father told Bhagat Singh that Mahatma Gandhi has said if these three young men were to be hanged, it should be done before the all India Congress session in Karachi. Bhagat Singh asked when the Karachi session was. His father said: "Towards the end of this month (March)." Bhagat Singh said it was then a matter of great rejoicing. Summer was approaching. It was better to die than get roasted in the cell. People said that after death one got a better life. "I shall be reborn in India. Perhaps I may have to face the British once again. My country should win independence," said Bhagat Singh.

Charat Singh indicated to him that the time allotted for the *mulaqat* (meeting) was over. He lingered back a bit. His family's love had overwhelmed him. He was pensive. Charat Singh told him to hurry up. His relatives embraced Bhagat Singh one by one to say goodbye. He touched his mother's feet. It was a gesture of reverence but it brought tears to the eyes of everyone. His sisters sobbed openly. Bhagat Singh was greatly upset. "Stay together," were his last words. He folded his hands as he retraced his steps.

On his way back to the cell, he saw Sukhdev and Rajguru still standing behind iron bars, forlorn and lonely. Despite Charat Singh's 'no', he stopped to chat with them. It would be any day, he told them. The last meeting with his family indicated that. They nodded in assent.

Many prisoners from nearby cells craned their necks for a glimpse of Bhagat Singh, the person they admired. They had come to know from Barkat, the jail barber, who flitted from one ward to another, that Bhagat Singh had had his *akhri mulaqat*. The hanging could not be very far.

Bhagat Singh found his shoulders wet. He recalled how Kultar wept incessantly. While saying goodbye, he had remarked: "Life will not be worth living without you." His grief-stricken face haunted Bhagat Singh. As the cell door closed behind him, he reached for his pen and wrote him a letter in Urdu, the language he normally used in personal letters.

Dear Kultar,

I was deeply grieved to see tears in your eyes. Your words today were full of pain. I cannot bear your tears. Darling, go on pursuing your studies with determination and take care of your health. Don't lose heart. What more can I say?

Let me recite some couplets. Lend me your ears.

Usay yeh fikr hai hardam naya tarze jafa kya hai,
Hamen yeh shauq hai dekhen sitam ki intiha kya hai
(Fresh avenues of fidelity are what my friend is seeking
but I want to experience the limits of tyranny.)
Mere hawa mein rahegi khayal ki khushboo,
Yeh mushte khaq hai, fani rahe na rahe.
(Our faith and ideas will fill the air.
What harm if this handful of dust is destroyed?)

It was a strange, smouldering love Bhagat Singh had for death. He often compared the execution of revolutionaries to a tryst with a beloved. Their lives too were a long wait, a quest for fulfilment.

They too burned in the fire of overpowering desire for sacrifice. Nothing could satiate them till they got what they cherished.

He believed that people like him must die to keep the torch of defiance burning. Revolutionaries were like tiny insects that hovered around a candle and threw themselves into the flame. He knew that his death was not far off. A couplet by Ghalib that Bhagat Singh used in the letter to Kultar was poignant.

Koi din ka mehman hun ai ahle mehfil

Chiraghe sehar hun bujha chahta hun

(Like the last flicker of lamp at dawn, I have but a few breaths of life left.)

Bhagat Singh did not think he was anyone special. He was one of thousands of people who, whatever their religion or region, were engaged in the same battle to free India. They had been thrown into the same cauldron. Together they were struggling and suffering for the cause. He had no doubt that they would emerge victorious one day.

After a revolutionary's arrest, the political significance of his action did not diminish, Bhagat Singh believed. Those who were arrested did not become more important than what they did. He and his two comrades were relevant to the extent that they got the opportunity to relay the message—to propagate and serve the cause of revolution. It was revolution that was important, not they.

The letter to Kultar was done. His words would soothe his brother, he hoped. But what about the millions of people who believed in him? They had given him more love than he deserved. They had followed him all through his hunger strikes, trials before magistrates and the Special Tribunal. They had supported him even when Gandhi had dismissed them as a bunch of 'misled' people, dictated by the cult of the bomb. He must reciprocate their love. He used the letter to Kultar to bid them goodbye. Once again he used an Urdu couplet to express himself.

Khush raho ahle watan hum to safar karte hain.

(Goodbye, dear countrymen, we proceed on a journey.)

After writing to his brother, Bhagat Singh reached for a notebook he maintained. It was neither a personal account nor a record of his reactions. Whatever struck him while reading a book, he noted that down. They were passages, mostly in English, by thinkers such as Aristotle, Plato, Descartes, Hobbes, Locke, Rousseau, Trotsky, Bertrand Russell, Karl Marx and Engels. Among the Indian authors he read were Rabindranath Tagore and Lajpat Rai. Bhagat Singh was also fond of poetry. He would recite even from Wordsworth, Byron and Omar Khayyam. But his favourite was Ghalib whom he quoted frequently.

His notebook began with an Urdu couplet:
Qurra-e-khalk hai gardish mein tapish se meri
Main woh Majnu hoon joh zindaan mein aazaad raha.

(The earth is rotating due to my free spirit. I am that lover, Majnu, who remained free even in the confines of a prison.)

The meeting with his family had shaken him emotionally. Although he had not forgiven his father for making a written request to the Tribunal saying that his son was innocent and that he had nothing to do with Saunders' murder, he knew his father was a sincere patriot who had devoted his life to the cause of independence. His father's filial affection at times had embarrassed Bhagat Singh as a revolutionary. But the way his father carried pain on his face was his way of saying sorry.

Bhagat Singh had chided him through a letter: "I have not been able to understand how you could think it proper to submit such a petition at this stage and in these circumstances...You know that in the political field my views have always differed with those of yours. I have always been acting independently without having cared for your approval or disapproval."

Bhagat Singh took the meeting with the family in his stride and immersed himself once again in books. He copied in the notebook an extract from Rousseau's novel, *Emile*, which he was reading before Charat Singh led him to the *mulaqat*.

"People think only of preserving their child's life; this is not enough; he must be taught to preserve his own life when he is a man, to bear the bullets of fortune, to brave wealth and poverty, to live at ease among the snows of Iceland or on the scorching rocks of Malta."

"Teach him to live, rather to avoid death. Life is not breath, but action. The use of our senses, our mind, our faculties, every part of ourselves which makes us conscious of our being. Life consists less in length of days than in a keen sense of living. A man may be buried at a hundred but may never have lived at all; he would have fared better had he died young."

A revolution could be achieved only through sustained striving, suffering and sacrifice. Bhagat Singh was content with the thought that there would be a revolution one day. He muttered: "Long live the revolution."

Ramanand Chatterji, editor of *Modern Review*, Calcutta, had ridiculed the slogan, Long Live the Revolution, and asked Bhagat Singh its exact meaning. Chatterji had written in an article: "When a desire is expressed for revolutions to live long, is it desired that the revolutionary process should be at work every hour, day, week, month and year of our lives? In other words, are we to have a revolution as often as possible?" Chatterji said that "a ceaseless revolutionary process would make India like what James Russell Lowell called 'the Catherine-wheel republics of South America' of his day. No doubt, no revolution can produce a final state of improvement; there must be change even after a revolution. But these should be brought about by evolution".

Bhagat Singh's reply was: "We are not the originators of this cry. The same cry had been used in the Russian revolutionary movements." He said that the phrase did not mean that sanguinary strife should ever continue, or that nothing should ever be stationary even for a short while. "By long usage this cry achieves a significance which may not be quite justifiable from the grammatical or the etymological point of view, but nevertheless we cannot abstract from that the association of ideas connected with that," he said.

The sense in which the word revolution had been used in that phrase, argued Bhagat Singh, "is the spirit, the longing for a change for the better. People generally get accustomed to the established order of things and begin to tremble at the very idea of a change. It is this lethargic spirit that needs to be replaced by the revolutionary spirit. Otherwise degeneration gains the upper hand and the whole humanity is led astray by the reactionary forces. Such a state of affairs leads to stagnation and paralysis in human progress. The spirit of revolution should always permeate the soul of humanity so that reactionary forces may not accumulate (strengthen) to check its eternal onward march. Old order should change, always and ever, yielding place to new, so that one 'good' order may not corrupt the world. It is in this sense that we raise the shout: Long Live Revolution".

With Chatterji, Bhagat Singh's confrontation was only on paper. He sent the reply four years after the article. However, his confrontation with Baba Randhir Singh, a freedom fighter detained in the same jail, was face to face, almost daily. Randhir Singh came to his cell one day to try to convince him about the existence of God. Bhagat Singh told him: "If, as you believe, there is an almighty, omnipresent, omniscient and omnipotent God, who created the earth or the world, please let me know why he created it. This world of miseries, an eternal combination of numberless tragedies: not a single human being is perfectly satisfied. Why does He not first produce a certain sentiment in the mind of the British people to liberate India?"

Randhir Singh was so angry that he nearly abused him: "You are giddy with fame and have developed an ego which is standing like a black curtain between you and God." Bhagat Singh was hurt. He wrote in reply a long article, 'Why I am an Atheist' (See Annexure 2). He resented the accusation. "I do not boast to be quite above these human traits. I am a man and nothing more. None can claim to be more. I have also this weakness in me. Vanity does form a part of my nature..."

Bhagat Singh was once a devout believer, an Arya Samajist although his father was a Sikh. Until his teenage years, he preserved his unshorn and unclipped long hair. But he could never believe in the mythology and doctrine of Sikhism or any other religion. By the time he came to shoulder the responsibility of revolutionary work, he had undergone a change.

In the name of God, Bhagat Singh recalled, Hindu-Muslim riots, broke out after the non-cooperation movement. He was horrified. How could the two communities who sank their religious differences and fought against the British to support the Caliphate in Turkey, thirst for each other's blood? Not that he believed it was a correct cause to take up. What disappointed him was the ferocity with which members of the two communities jumped at each other's throats after sharing the same platforms, the same campaigns and even the same jails.

Here were thousands of people, who agitated side by side for days but had turned into enemies overnight. It was strange, that they participated in the movement yet remained strangers. They never fought as Indians, not even as human beings. Religious, political or personal considerations brought them together. But at heart, they remained biased and bigoted, only Hindus and Muslims.

In contrast, ideology bound the revolutionaries. Even a one-day agitation revealed their kinship. Their commitment tied them together. They were on the same wavelength. They were against importing religion and its idioms to the struggle for independence.

No more mysticism, no more blind faith. Realism became the cult. He studied Bakunin, the anarchist leader, much of Lenin, Trotsky, and others. They were all atheists. He came across a book, *Common Sense*, by Nirlamba Swami. It was a sort of mystic atheism.

Bhagat Singh went along with Gandhi as far as his fight against the British was concerned. But he could not support him on all counts. Gandhi had a knack of mixing religion with popular movements. True, it aroused a wide response but in the process it also sowed religious feelings in the minds of people which came in the way of secular ethos. Ram Rajya was a concept of an ideal state in Hindu religion. It was like Plato's Republic, not attainable. But terms like Ram Rajya sowed suspicion in the minds of minorities as if Hindu ideology was being imposed on them. Such terminology unnecessarily created doubts. A pluralistic society required a secular approach; even a bit of bias could contaminate the nation.

It seemed strange to him that the revolutionaries, who fought against prejudice all their lives, fell victim to it before dying. He had in mind some of the UP comrades in the Kakori case. That they funded revolutionary activities through dacoities was acceptable to him as it was acceptable to Chandra Shekhar Azad and some of his other comrades. Ram Prasad Bismil and Ashfhaqullah Khan had entered a train carrying a government *tajori* (strong box) on August 9, 1925, at Shahjahanpur, and pulled the chain at a wayside railway station, Kakori, between Hardoi and Shahjahanpur. They fired their revolvers to create confusion and then captured the *tajori*. (So strongly was it built that muscular Ashfhaqullah had to use a hammer to break it open.) Bhagat Singh appreciated their bravery.

He also saw a point in the argument that there was no harm in looting the government treasury, which was, after all, filled by extracting hard-earned money from the Indians. But he could not understand why Bismil and Ashfhagullah* decided to highlight their religious identities, and not the revolutionaries' creed of secularism before the hanging. Ashfhaqullah went to the gallows with the Koran dangling from his neck and Bismil the Gita. Why did they have to do so? Before the execution, Ashfhaqullah—an

*The British managed to arrest most of the Kakori case revolutionaries. Some were hanged and some given life imprisonment.

Urdu poet as he was—had even recited one of his couplets which reflected his patriotic sentiments, not religious.

Kuchh arzoo nahi hai, Hai arzoo to yeh
Rakhde koi zarasi khake watan kafan mein.

(I have no desire. If at all there is one, it is that someone should place the earth of my country in the coffin.)

Bhagat Singh wondered. He recalled how the first revolutionary he came in contact with would not dare to deny the existence of God. He would say: "Pray whenever you want to." This was like riding two horses at the same time. Why could people not believe that religion made people accept the status quo because God ordained it that way, Bhagat Singh felt. How could promoters of change believe in the inevitability of holy books?

Bhagat Singh had found to his dismay that in the early days revolutionaries in Bengal were recruited exclusively from Hindu middle classes. In fact, the revolutionary groups were recognisably anti-Muslim. Since the British government tended to use Muslims against the national struggle—and many Muslims played the establishment's game—they were suspect in the eyes of the revolutionaries.

When East Bengal was sought to be made into a separate province, Bamfield Fuller, then the Lieutenant Governor, openly said that the government looked upon the Muslim community as its "favourite wife". The remark rubbed the revolutionaries the wrong way. They felt that the Muslims were an obstacle in the way of India's freedom and must, like other obstacles, be removed.

One other factor was responsible for the dislike of Muslims by the Bengali revolutionaries. The British felt that they could not trust Bengali employees fully in dealing with revolutionary activities because they were 'politically awake'. What had happened was that Muslim employees from UP were brought to man the intelligence branch of the Bengal police. The result was that the Hindus of Bengal began to feel that Muslims were against political freedom and against the Hindu community as such.

For Bhagat Singh, a revolutionary was not super human. He was conscious of his frailties. And he fought them relentlessly and tried to overcome them. But how could he fall prey to bigotry? Idealism bound him by conviction and commitment and gave him power to devise methods to attain the objective. While immersed in society, he transcended it. If he could not rise above bias or prejudice, he failed to be a revolutionary.

Bhagat Singh flipped the pages of his notebook and read a quotation from Bertrand Russell slowly: "My own view of religion is that of Lucretin. I regard it as a disease born of fear and as a source of untold misery to the human race. I cannot, however, deny that it has made some contribution to civilisation. It helped in early days to fix the calendar and it caused the Egyptian priests to chronicle eclipses with such care that in time they became able to predict them. These two services, I am prepared to acknowledge but I do not know of any other."

Bhagat Singh could not push back Kultar's tearful face from his mind. How could he explain to his brother that life was not words, but action, the use of our senses, our mind, every part of ourselves. He remembered that he had yet to copy in his notebook a quote by James Russell Lowell. Bhagat Singh captioned it, 'Freedom'.

...True Freedom is to share
All the chains our brothers wear,
And, with heart and hand, to be
Earnest to make others free.

They are slaves who fear to speak
For the fallen and the weak;
They are slaves who will not choose
Hatred, scoffing and abuse,
Rather than in silence shrink.
From the truth they need must think;
They are slaves who dare not be
In the right with two or three.

Going through the pages of the notebook, Bhagat Singh's eyes got fixed on a sentence he had reproduced from the writings of Lajpat Rai. "No rule over a foreign people is so exacting and so merciless in its operation as that of democracy." The words brought before him a multitude of memories. He recalled how in response to Gandhi's call to boycott the Simon Commission he had joined the demonstration against it.

Two

It was October 3, 1928. Some 5,000 protestors had gathered near Lahore railway station, demonstrating against a seven-man commission, led by Sir John Allsbrook Simon. The members had arrived from London via Bombay. The task assigned to them was to assess whether and how far India was 'ready for further constitutional reforms'. It was a statutory obligation which the British had to fulfil every 10 years under the Indian Council Act, 1919, known as the Montague-Chelmsford Reforms. The intent was to 'help' India move towards 'self-rule', whatever that meant.

Gandhi was conscious of the limitations of the Congress. Still he believed the British would offer Dominion Status. And he was confident that he could bring the Congress around to accept it, although the party had threatened to go the whole hog for independence if Dominion Status was not granted by December 31, 1929. But the Commission's appointment was an anti-climax. It meant, Gandhi began to feel, that the British were not serious about giving India any substantial powers. They were only playing with the sentiments of the Indian people.

He had gone to the farthest limit to cooperate with them in the step-by-step approach involved in the transfer of power. He felt so let down that he persuaded the Congress, which looked to him for guidance, to pass a resolution declaring that the only self-respecting course of action for India to adopt was to boycott the commission at every stage and in every form.

The Congress was his instrument. When founded in 1885 by a Briton, Allan Octavian Hume, the party was Her Majesty's loyal organisation. In the earlier years, the party awaited favours from the rulers like crumbs from the dining table of the rich. The Congress was then a tool in the hands of the British to hoodwink Indian public opinion. The rulers directed it from behind the scenes. For the Indian elite, the Congress was a club through which they kept contact with those who mattered in the establishment.

Whenever London thought of associating the natives with power at some tier of governance, it sought the Congress first. The elite knew it and flocked to the Congress. The British found the party handy and obedient. But with the passage of time, it too had been awakened by liberal ideology. Self-rule whetted the appetite for more self-rule. The Congress showed signs of 'impudence'. But still it was under the influence of the British.

After Bal Gangadhar Tilak, who famously declared that "freedom is my birthright", it was Gandhi who had infused life—and rebellion—into the body politic of India. After his return from South Africa, where he had won several non-violent battles for the rights of Indians settled there, he found the Congress the best platform to experiment with his ideas. Gandhi was no revolutionary of the Bhagat Singh-type. He did not speak the language of fire and brimstone. Nor was he willing to rub the British on the wrong side. His was a cooperative approach. But he had his own plan of action, to achieve things peacefully, without the use of violence either in methods or words. Non-violence was the most deadly weapon he had because it killed the opponent by setting his own example to suffer, not to retaliate.

The radicals did not accept his philosophy. To them he was a visionary but not a person who could make the British afraid. Yet they had to reckon with his leadership because he had charisma. The teeming millions in India followed him.

The greatest defect in radical socialists, according to Gandhi's next-in-command, Jawaharlal Nehru, was their contempt for what might be called the moral and spiritual side of life. Their philosophy not only ignored something basic in man, but also deprived human behaviour of standards and values. Ethical aspects, he said, "are ultimately basic to culture and civilisation" which gave some meaning to life. Nehru strongly believed Gandhi's dictum that "wrong means will not lead to right results".

The revolutionaries knew that their thinking did not tally with that of Gandhi. The experience of a century-long and worldwide struggle between the masses and the governing class, was their guide to their goal, and the methods they were following "had never been known to have failed". Before them the French Revolution had successfully proclaimed the ideas of liberty, fraternity and equality, while the Bolshevik Revolution had introduced the ideas of socialism.

Bhagat Singh and his comrades did not support Dominion Status. Their demand was for full independence. Still they decided to respond to Gandhi's call to boycott the Simon Commission. As revolutionaries, they believed that any move to stir people was a step in the right direction. Such a step, however small, would make the nation conscious of the shackles it wore. Action, action was the soul of success in revolution. Gandhi stood for the humble. They recalled how at an ostentatious *pandal* he had said: "When millions are not able to feed themselves even once a day, how could they indulge in such excesses?"

As soon as the commission members stepped out of the railway station porch, the crowd surged forward. This was the first time that the protestors had raised the slogan *Inquilab Zindabad*. Bhagat Singh had coined it to give the freedom struggle a new edge, a new meaning, that of revolt, of defiance.

The crowd raised slogans: "Simon Commission go back" and "*Angrez Murdabad*" (Down with the British). People also chanted a rhyme:

Hindustani hain hum, Hindustan hamara
Mur jao Simon jahan hai desh tumhara.

(We are Indians and India is ours, Go back Simon to the country to which you belong).

Lala Lajpat Rai was at the forefront of the protestors. Bhagat Singh had differences with him because it was Lalaji who had authored the idea that India should be divided into two countries: Hindu India and Muslim India. Bhagat Singh could not contemplate such a partition. Hindus and Muslims had been living side by side in thousands of towns, villages and hamlets for hundreds of years. They shared each other's sorrow and happiness, heritage and history. They toiled together and suffered together. The entire country belonged to both the communities. When free, they would shape the country's destiny, political and economic, together as equal participants in the task of nation-building.

Bhagat Singh, for one, had many Muslim comrades. They were like him. They ate the same food, wore the same clothes, spoke the same language and reacted in the same manner. Just because the Muslims followed a different religion from his, it did not make them different. They were no aliens. They were the warp and woof of the same fabric that constituted the Indian nation. Why should they give up what was their patrimony and content themselves with a mere fragment of it? How could religion separate them from the Hindus?

Bhagat Singh feared that if Lajpat Rai's idea of a division of the country along religious lines ever took shape, it would be disastrous. There would be a bloodbath. Hindu and Muslim countries would be perpetually at war. All their attention and resources would be diverted towards acquiring weapons to fight one another. Religion, he felt, was the prop of a man who had not yet found himself.

With Lajpat Rai, Bhagat Singh had joined issue more than once. He had regretted his tilt towards Hindu chauvinism. Lajpat Rai, in turn, had denounced him as a 'Russian Agent'. He regarded revolutionaries as 'irresponsible' young men.

Yet Bhagat Singh had deep respect for Lajpat Rai. Lalaji's life-long fight against the British was a sterling example before the country. He had been banished to Burma for his anti-British activities. Whatever his weak points, he was a great man. He had served the country well. His sacrifices and defiance of rulers had trailed a path for the youth. Bhagat Singh was opposed to Lajpat Rai's parochialism. But he bowed his head before Lalaji's patriotism, and devotion to India. Bhagat Singh curbed his misgivings and rallied behind Lajpat Rai.

The crowd stood like a wall. It prevented the members of the commission from moving forward. A large contingent of policemen tried to push people back to clear the way. They did not budge. Lajpat Rai, in an impromptu speech, said: "If the government did not wish the commission to see the demonstrators, the best thing for it to do was to put blindfolds over the eyes of members and take them straight to the government house."

Superintendent of Police J.A. Scott ordered a lathi-charge. The crowd ran helter-skelter. Some fell by the roadside, some braved the lathi-charge and some were arrested. Still many stood their ground. Lajpat Rai exhorted them to hold to their position like true *satyagrahis* (truth warriors). Many returned. They were his flock and he their shepherd.

Scott spotted Lajpat Rai from a distance and went for him. The policeman used his baton to beat the Indian leader mercilessly and did not stop even when blood began spurting from Lajpat Rai's chest. Scott did not stop till Lalaji fell down. It looked as if Scott was releasing his pent-up anger against all those who defied the British. He looked like an Englishman who wanted to teach a lesson to the crowd, to let it know the fate of those who challenged the authority of the British.

Only nine years earlier, Brigadier-General Reginald Dyer, an Irishman born in Simla, had wreaked his vengeance upon the people of Amritsar for heckling a British woman in one of the city's bazars. He too was motivated by the sentiment to set an example, and to let the natives realise what the Raj would do to make them fall in line.

Dyer, who was given control of Amritsar by Lieutenant Governor of Punjab Michael O'Dwyer, chose April 13, 1919, the day of the Punjab harvest festival, *Baisakhi*, for his revenge. To voice their protest against the Rowlatt Act, which gave the rulers the power to detain anyone without trial, some 20,000 people had collected in a garden, called Jallianwala Bagh, a stone's throw from the Golden Temple.

Dyer set the police on the gathering like hunters unchaining their ferocious hounds to bring the pursued animal to bay. He purposely blocked the garden's only gate to prevent anyone from escaping from the place. He wanted the Indians to remember what could happen when the rulers decided to act. Targeted by machine guns, men, women and children had no escape or respite from the bullets till the police exhausted their ammunition. As many as 1,650 rounds were fired. Scores of people jumped into the garden's only well, mute witnesses to that barbarous massacre. Some 400 people died on the spot and more than 1,500 were injured.

London too was horrified. It recalled Dyer who, appearing before an inquiry committee, said that he had done his duty. He expressed no regret. Nor was he admonished. Some in the British political hierarchy rationalised that he had saved Punjab from 'anarchy'.

Bhagat Singh had visited the hallowed place and carried in his pocket for a long time a packet of dust he had collected from there. This was his way of paying homage to those who had been killed by the rulers. Dyer got away with his barbarous deed, Scott must not. Bhagat Singh was determined that Scott should be made to pay for the insult he had heaped on Indians.

Lajpat Rai fell on the ground, bleeding profusely and moaning loudly. Before he lost consciousness, he shouted: "Every blow that was hurled at us this afternoon was a nail in the coffin of the British Empire." How prophetic were his words—Britain's rule ended 18 years later, on August 15, 1947. He said: "I wish to warn the government that if a violent revolution takes place in this country, the responsibility for bringing it about will fall on such officers as misbehaved themselves today."

Not far from the railway station ground, where Lajpat Rai lay wounded, was the river Ravi. Jawaharlal Nehru had unfurled on the river bank the tricolour*, the Congress party flag, on January 26, 1930, to make an unambiguous declaration that India would not accept anything less than full independence (Purna Swaraj). Bhagat Singh and other revolutionaries felt vindicated that their pressure had compelled Gandhi to extend the demand beyond Dominion Status. Gandhi too, on his own, had come to the conclusion that the British would not transfer any meaningful power to India. Three years earlier, he had pulled up Nehru for having sponsored a resolution for independence. Now he himself gave a call to celebrate January 26 as a day for Purna Swaraj.

Seeing Lajpat Rai falling, a wave of horror and indignation swept through the crowd. Nobody could imagine that the British would beat a person of his stature like a criminal. Bhagat Singh could not believe that a *gora* (white man) would dare to take a baton in his hand and pounce upon Lajpat Rai.

As the news of Lajpat Rai's injuries spread, anger gripped the country. Gandhi said: "What I would like the workers to draw from this incident is not to be depressed or taken aback by assault, but to treat it as part of the game. We have to turn the irritation caused by the unwarranted assault into dynamic energy and translate it for future purposes." Nehru asked the British to take concrete steps to atone for the insult to the nation. He described the tragedy as a national humiliation.

How helpless were the Indians! They could not even protect the honour of their chosen leaders. The Lajpat Rai incident brought

---

*The idea came to Gandhi that the Indian flag should be white, green and red—white representing purity, green representing the Muslims and red representing the Hindus—and that there should be a spinning wheel in the middle because 'India as a nation can live and die only for the spinning wheel.' Seventeen years later a flag replacing the spinning wheel with the Ashok Chakra was adopted as the national flag of India.

matters to a head. It made the nation more indignant than ever before.

The anger that Bhagat Singh had felt after visiting Jallianwala Bagh welled up again when he saw Lajpat Rai on the ground. He swore to avenge the insult but he wanted to discuss with his comrades the punishment they should mete out to the cruel rulers. They had a retreat at Mozang Road in Lahore. It was a non-descript, rented building, close to a burial ground, away from the gaze of the police. They met there practically every day. Today was no different.

Rajguru and Sukhdev, the·two senior members of the revolutionary party, the HSRA, were already discussing Scott's. arrogance when Bhagat Singh stepped in. They were aware of the brutal lathi-charge and the injuries inflicted on Lajpat Rai. Bhagat Singh narrated to them the entire incident and expressed fear that the "Lion of Punjab," as Lajpat Rai was known, might not live long.

How to take revenge was the topic of discussion among the three. One suggestion was to involve the police in a pitched battle, as Jatindra Nath Mukherjee, a revolutionary from Bengal, had done earlier. It happened during the First World War when he was taking delivery of arms from the German cruiser, *Emden*, on the eastern Indian coast. Four young revolutionaries were with him None of them knew that armed policemen had been following them. When they came to know about it, they confronted the force at Balasore, Orissa. The revolutionaries had no other option. Their ammunition was running short and their chance of escaping was nil, since they were surrounded from all sides.

Outnumbered and outgunned, they went on shooting till the shower of police bullets took a dreadful toll. Seeing them grievously injured, the British officers called a halt to the operation. Two of them went forward. None of the revolutionaries disclosed Mukherjee's name, even when the British assured them that the purpose was only to render them medical assistance. Chittapriya, fatally hurt, told them not to disturb him and to let him die peacefully. The two others also died later. So struck were the two British officers by the bravery of these Bengali revolutionaries that they honoured the dead by firing into the air.

Bhagat Singh said that a pitched battle with the police was no revenge against Scott, who was the culprit. "Blood for blood." This was the message they wanted to convey to London. Ten Englishmen would die for every Hindustani they killed, Bhagat Singh said. The formal decision was deferred till the meeting of the HSRA. Chandra Shekhar Azad, head of its armed unit, who was still underground after the Kakori train hold-up case, was sent an urgent message to return to Lahore.

Lajpat Rai died on November 17. Before dying, he warned the British that if incidents like the one at Lahore continued to happen, "I would not wonder if the young men go out of our hands and do whatever they choose with the object of gaining the freedom of heir country". Indeed, they were already losing faith in Gandhi's methods which, they described as "midsummer night's dreams".

The revolutionaries were in an ugly mood when they met on the night of December 10. Durga Devi, affectionately called Durga Bhabi, presided over the meeting. As the wife of the party's ideologue and the author of the HSRA's manifesto, Bhagwati Charan Vohra, she was also respected as a revolutionary in her own right. She was once imprisoned for three years in a shooting case.

The meeting decided unanimously to kill Scott. Since he was responsible for Lajpat Rai's death, he must pay with his life. The revolutionaries had several things in mind. They also wanted to give credence to their dictum of the adopting violent struggle when it became necessary. They expected to awaken the young from the drudgery of slavery and to participate in the revolutionary struggle against foreign domination and economic exploitation.

Bhagat Singh and his associates proposed to show the world that India would not suffer evil and nor would the country accept Lajpat Rai's death lying down. Rajguru repeated his earlier proposal of challenging the police and sacrificing themselves while fighting. Such a heroic, dare-devil act would fire the imagination of the youth and swell their number in the HSRA. The proposal was again vigorously rejected because the purpose was to target Lajpat Rai's killer.

Reviewing the situation in the country, Bhagat Singh said that there was on all pervading sense of tension. The Bengal party had done a commendable job. It had killed some officials forcing many terror-stricken Englishmen to send their families back to England. Soon they would realise that India would not remain with them. "The blood of the young men was boiling," he said.

Durga Devi first asked for volunteers to kill Scott and then raised her hand. Nobody was willing to involve her. They recognised her commitment to revolution. She had stood by them under all circumstances. But they could not think of exposing her to risk when all of them were willing to sacrifice their lives. It was not male chauvinism. She was their *bhabhi*, wife of their revered comrade who had gone out of Lahore. Reluctantly, she ruled herself out and asked for volunteers.

Bhagat Singh, Sukhdev, Rajguru and Chandra Shekhar, as well as nearly all those present, raised their hands. Durga Devi looked towards Sukhdev, who was their strategist. He provided them with ideas. Sukhdev wanted the assignment for himself. But he was ruled out. He was the kingpin of the network which strung together revolutionaries in different parts of the country, particularly the Punjab, the cradle of their activity. He was the planner. He accepted, however, the role of arbiter. He then chose four comrades from among those present: Bhagat Singh, Rajguru, Chandra Shekhar Azad, and Jai Gopal.

Chalking out the operation, Sukhdev said that Bhagat Singh would be the one to kill Scott. Sukhdev was certain that the task would be executed once it was entrusted to him. As soon as Bhagat Singh's name was announced, there were whispers in the room, some suspecting that Sukhdev wanted to get rid of him because of his growing popularity. Shooting Scott was difficult, but escaping from the police dragnet would be impossible.

Sukhdev behaved as if he had not heard the whispers. He spelled out the rest of his plan to kill Scott. Rajguru was selected to stand near Bhagat Singh to give him protection. The third person, Azad, was to arrange their escape. Jai Gopal, a relatively junior comrade, had a simple errand—to let the three know when Scott arrived at the police station.

December 17 was fixed as the date for Scott's assassination. On December 15, the four men met to rehearse their assignments. By this time, each one was familiar with the role he had to play. Bhagat Singh had even thought of the exact spot where he would shoot down Scott. Azad explained to Bhagat Singh and Rajguru how they would escape.

Bhagat Singh prepared a red-lettered poster: SCOTT KILLED. Little did he realise then that one day his handwritten poster would be used as evidence against him in the courts. Nor did he suspect that Hans Raj Vohra, a quiet young man who prepared three or four copies of the poster, would one day turn government approver.

Bhagat Singh was very particular about bringing in the name of the armed wing of the HSRA in whatever action they undertook. He said that the notice they issued after Scott's murder would carry the name of the HSRA army. "Our party has a strong military wing," he would proudly say. He wanted the armed wing to be a recognisable force in the minds of the youth so that they would put faith in it as the body which would one day challenge the British army and smash the exploitative imperial system.

For the HSRA, Bhagat Singh had cut his hair and shaved off his beard. This was the party's order to its members in order to defy detection by the police. The decision was taken at the Ferozeshah Kotla meeting when the different units decided to merge into the HSRA. He went to Ferozepur in the middle of September, 1928 and hired a medical practitioner to cut his hair. Jai Gopal was with him.

Jai Gopal was the one deputed to identify Scott. But he had never seen the Englishman before. Strangely, Jai Gopal did not tell this to anybody. For him, it was such a prestigious assignment that he did not want to lose it. That he made a mess of it was another matter.

On December 17, Scott did not come to the police station. He took leave because he had to receive his mother-in-law who was arriving from England. Jai Gopal mistook Assistant Superintendent of Police J.P. Saunders for Scott and informed the three about his arrival at the police station at 10 a.m. A few hours later, they took positions and waited for the time when he would depart.

In the afternoon, when Saunders came out of the police station and reached for his motorcycle, Rajguru shot him with his German Mauser pistol. Bhagat Singh shouted: "No, no, he is not the man". But was too late. By then, Rajguru had killed him, an excellent shot that he was. His one bullet had done the job. Bhagat Singh too pumped bullets from his pistol into the dead body.*

As planned beforehand, Bhagat Singh and Rajguru ran towards DAV College, a few yards away from the police station. Azad had positioned himself in such a way that he could give them cover. A British officer, Inspector W.J.C. Fern, emerged from the police station on hearing the commotion. But he quickly retraced his steps when two bullets shot by Azad whizzed past his head.

Head Constable Chanan Singh, who heard the shots, ran out to help Saunders. He was the only one who chased Bhagat Singh,

*The post-mortem confirmed this.

Rajguru and Azad as they ran from the place where Saunders lay dead. "No, we do not want to kill an Indian," Azad shouted. But Chanan Singh did not stop. Rajguru shot him dead. Many people watched the scene from the windows of nearby buildings. The revolutionary Urdu poet, Faiz Ahmad Faiz, was one of them.

The three revolutionaries entered the compound of DAV College. Then they scaled a wall which divided the college from the hostel. They stopped for a while at the hostel. When they found that no one was pursuing them, they walked out at a normal pace. They picked up their bicycles, which Azad had placed against the hostel toilet wall. Once again, they checked all directions to ensure their safety. When they found no one on their trail, they pedalled leisurely to their retreat, the Mozang Road house.

A police party appeared long after they had left. The boarding house was surrounded. A roll call of residents was taken. Every room was searched. The police also ransacked the college. But it found no trace of the culprits. The Punjab government informed the Home Department: "Saunders, Assistant Superintendent Police, was shot down and killed this afternoon by two youths who escaped into the DAV College and then into the country on bicycles..."

By the time the authorities came to know of Saunders' murder, all the three revolutionaries were comfortably sitting at the Mozang Road house and comparing notes. After informing them that Scott had reached the police station, Jai Gopal had gone home. They could not even chide him that his mistake had led to the murder of Saunders instead of Scott.

Practically every policeman in Lahore was put on duty to find the killers. All roads and railway exits from the city were heavily guarded. The authorities suspected the hand of the revolutionaries. But they could not put their finger on the main culprits or how they had vanished.

The news of Saunders' death spread in no time. Posters appeared at several places in Lahore. The most prominent was the one on which Bhagat Singh had hurriedly printed Saunders' name over that of Scott. The poster read:

HINDUSTAN SOCIALIST REPUBLICAN ARMY NOTICE

   J.P. Saunders is dead; Lala Lajpat Rai is avenged

"Really it is horrible to imagine that so lowly and violent hand of an ordinary police official, J.P. Saunders, could ever dare to touch in such an insulting way the body of one so old, so revered and so loved by 300 million people of Hindustan and thus cause his death. The youth and manhood of India was challenged by blows hurled down on the head of India's nationhood. And let the world know that India still lives; that the blood of youths has not been totally cooled down and that they can still risk their lives, if the honour of their nation is at stake. And it is proved through this act by those obscure who are ever persecuted, condemned and denounced even by their own people."

Beware, Ye Tyrants; Beware

"Do not injure the feelings of a downtrodden and oppressed country. Think twice before perpetrating such diabolical deeds. And remember that despite the 'Arms Act' and strict guards against the smuggling of arms, the revolvers will ever continue to flow in—if not sufficient at present for an armed revolt, then at least sufficient to avenge the national insults. In spite of all the denunciations and condemnation of their own kith and kin, and ruthless repression and persecution of the alien government, the party of young men will ever live to teach a lesson to the haughty rulers. They will be so bold as to cry even amidst the raging storm of opposition and repression, even on the scaffold."

Long Live The Revolution

"Sorry for the death of a man. But in this man has died the representative of an institution which is so cruel, lowly and so base that it must be abolished. In this man has died an agent of the British authority in India—the most tyrannical of government of governments in the world.

Sorry for the bloodshed of a human being; but the sacrifice of individuals at the altar of the Revolution that will bring freedom to all and make the exploitation of man by man impossible, is inevitable."

Long Live The Revolution

Dated 18th December, 1928   Sd/-Balraj
Commander-In-Chief.

Sitting at the Mozang Road house, the three considered several options to escape from Lahore which they imagined would be swarming with police. They thought they would hide for some time and surface again. After all, the only person who had seen them was Head Constable Chanan Singh and he was dead. There was no witness to identify them.

Still something told them that Lahore was not a safe place. The police would tighten its dragnet and it was only a matter of time before they would be caught. Bhagat Singh's hunch was that the police must already be combing the city for the revolutionaries and even knocking at the doors of sympathisers. Too many of them were staying scattered across too many places. Someone, somewhere might spill the beans and tell the police all about them and their hideouts. They could not afford to put others in jeopardy. They must quit the city immediately.

Strangely, they had planned the assassination meticulously but had paid little attention to their escape. It spoke well of their bravery, but not of their strategy. They had no clue about what to do. But they felt relieved when Sukhdev stepped in. He was conscious of their predicament.

He told them how to escape. They must go to Durga Devi and do what he had said. But Sukhdev also insisted that they leave Lahore quickly. They had to wait. They knew her house was under police surveillance from 11 p.m. to 5 a.m. Till then, they had to wait at the Mozang Road house. But they had no money.

Bhagat Singh felt confident enough to run up to a nearby post office to find a friend or sympathiser who would give him some cash. He saw Sohan Singh Josh, an old communist, there. Josh commended the job. But he told Bhagat Singh not to visit any public place for some days. Bhagat Singh returned empty-handed.

It was still dark when he, Rajguru and Chandra Shekhar Azad used the wheat fields behind Mozang Road to go to Durga Devi's house. It was numbingly cold. Frost covered the fields, making it appear like a white sheet. And it was so quiet that they could hear the sound of their own footsteps, trampling upon the newly sprung crop. Some farmers were already in their fields, a few pouring water on their bodies and a few were at the plough. The countryside was beginning to wake up to the jingling of cattle-bells, the gurgling of water from Persian wells and the squeaking of poorly-oiled wooden carts.

Fields always had a great impact on Bhagat Singh. They reminded him of his roots, his rural background. He thought of the time when wheat and other agricultural produce came to their home. His mother was generous to those who toiled on their land. He had suggested to his father more than once to give the land to those who ploughed it. His father was furious with him. But Bhagat Singh stuck to his belief that the land belonged to those who tilled and tended it.

After spending many years in the village, Bhagat Singh's family moved to a suburb of Lahore, Nehrankot, where his father took up the insurance business. Bhagat Singh joined a DAV school, an usual choice for a Sikh school boy, who would, as custom dictated, have gone to a Khalsa school. But then his father had never believed in sectarian education, which he believed only inculcated the bigoted aspect of religion. It was not the approach of religious tolerance which Bhagat Singh's family followed.

A little after five in the morning, when the police departed from outside Durga Devi's house, Bhagat Singh and his two comrades knocked at her door. It was too early for her to expect a visitor. She felt concerned. She hesitated before unbolting the door. To her pleasant surprise, Bhagat Singh stood before her. As he stepped in, Rajguru and Azad followed him. She congratulated them for a job well done. They tried to explain to her that by mistake they had killed Saunders in place of Scott. She knew all about it. But this in no way minimised their act of courage, she said.

They told her about Sukhdev's advice and their decision to escape from Lahore that very day. Then they unfolded the plan to travel by train to Calcutta where her husband had gone to attend the All India Congress Committee's annual session. But they had no money. She brought 500 rupees, which Bhagwati Charan had left behind. Would they be able to go by train unrecognised? They had their doubts. The police would be in full strength at the station. But then there was no alternative. They had to take a risk.

The Dehra Dun Express leaving for Calcutta in the morning, as Sukhdev had suggested, was their best bet. Azad had his own plan and left the house. There was no time to lose. Sukhdev had worked out the details: Bhagat Singh would act as Durga Devi's husband. She herself suggested the name, Ranjit. She called herself Sujatha. Her three-year-old boy, Sachin, would be their child. Rajguru would act as their servant.

Bhagat Singh, dressed as a government official, wore Bhagwati Charan's overcoat and sported a felt hat, which someone had left behind at his house several months before. Rajguru fetched a *tonga* and put their luggage in it. The boxes were labelled as was the practice among government officials. No policeman was around yet. Bhagat Singh was sure that no government official had yet connected him or Rajguru with the killing. He was right. Bhagat Singh and his comrades were not suspects, though there was a firm belief in the government that it was the handiwork of the revolutionaries. But there was no evidence to corroborate their participation. Posters by the HSRA army confirmed the hand of the revolutionaries. But that was all.

Lahore railway station was like a fortress, swarming with policemen. First class passengers had to disclose their names. Bhagat Singh bought a ticket and muttered some name.

A couple, the husband dressed in European clothes and the wife in her sari with high heels clicking, walked confidently to the first class compartment. They were trailed by a servant, carrying a child. There was such a flourish about them that the police did not dare accost them. "They are sahibs," policemen guarding the train said. He must be a high government official, some policemen at a distance whispered. Bhagat Singh and his party were left alone. The Dehra Dun Express chugged out of Lahore slowly, some white men lingering on the platform, waving or raising their handkerchiefs to their wives and children.

Azad, after leaving Durga Devi's house, joined a party of pilgrims going to Mathura to offer prayers at Lord Krishna's temple. While singing *bhajans*, they passed a group of policemen who did not even care to stop them and check their identities.

The three in the train felt satisfied that they had played their part well. They had not aroused even an iota of suspicion. For a short time they were tense. But as the train speeded up, they felt confident. Indeed, they had eluded the police. Still, to be doubly sure that they were not being followed, they decided to get down at Kanpur.

Bhagat Singh looked out of the window to see the countryside. He felt the spirit of India, a land of struggle and sacrifice, of suffering and subjugation, where people had defended their identity, their being, against all odds for centuries.

Raiders came and retreated. Empires grew and tumbled down. Dynasties rose and fell. India was conquered and re-conquered, destroyed and disfigured. But it remained alive. Foreign regimes were like a gale that passed over its head, seldom disturbing the country's rhythm of life, moral codes and values. Kings and kingdoms were never able to intrude upon the people's privacy, their reflective thinking or their innate dignity.

Time was a mute witness to the spell that India cast on the outsiders who came to enslave it but who eventually made it their home. The slave dynasty or the Mughals, all were absorbed in a composite society, as the Buddhists and the Jains had been centuries earlier. Over the years, the rulers and the ruled became part and parcel of the same tapestry, drawing strength from the different threads that were interwoven into the fabric of the country, resulting in a texture which reflected diverse shades in a smooth and sturdy fashion. What held people together was not religion, race or language but a commitment to a certain way of life. It was a shared experience of involvement and the spirit of tolerance and accommodation.

And as the Ganga had taken into her lap a multitude of streams, whether stormy, placid or dirty, so too had India assimilated the strange and the strong from several lands. Both the river and the country were not defiled, and remained pure. There was music and dance, but also the clash of swords and the exchange of gunfire. Despite this, what filled the atmosphere was gentle harmony matched by patience. To Bhagat Singh's regret, patience made the people accept even their poverty with noble resignation. They attributed their plight to *kismat* (fate). He blamed Gandhi for encouraging such a sense of resignation among the people.

The three broke their journey at Kanpur and stayed at a hotel near the station. Durga Devi sent a telegram to her husband, informing him of her arrival, accompanied by her brother.

The next morning, they boarded a train for Calcutta. So far Bhagat Singh had exchanged few words with Durga Devi. He was busy assimilating India. Now he wanted to tell her everything about himself, especially how he had taken the road to revolution. He was then studying at National College in Lahore, founded by some nationalist Punjabis who wished to spread the message of nationalism among the youth of the province. Bhimsen Sachar, who later became the Chief Minister of Punjab, was the Registrar. The revolutionary minded Chabildas was the principal who lectured the students on patriotism. His favourite quatrain was:

Duniya se ghulami ka mein nam mita dunga
Ik bar zamane ko mein azad kara dunga
Jo log gharibon par kartein hain sitam nahaq
Gar dam hai mera kayam gin gin ke saza dunga

(I shall obliterate the name of slavery from the world. I will free the universe. I shall punish so long as I live each one of them who heap cruelties on the poor without reason.)

Bhagat Singh admitted to Durga Devi that he deplored the outrages which accompanied revolutionary violence. But the more violent the outrages, the more assured he felt that a revolution was necessary. He told her that Shachindranath Sanyal, a Bengali revolutionary, a student at National College, warned him that he would be able to imbibe the spirit of revolution only when he left home. Yashpal, a fiery Hindi writer, also at his college, told him that as long as men led purely private lives with their families, they would be prisoners of natural impulses. They were not really free. They were too bogged down of emotional ties. They must think of society as the whole; in fact of mankind. They must go out into the world and play their part on the stage of history.

Durga Devi knew Sukhdev as a cold strategist. She wanted to know from Bhagat Singh how he became close to Sukhdev. He said he had met Sukhdev at National College. They became friends at their first meeting. So strong was their friendship that they never separated for the rest of their lives.

Bhagat Singh recalled that both of them would discuss endlessly India's political condition and the lack of revolutionary zeal, without which they did not see an early release from British domination or the capitalist system. They exchanged notes on books which they freely borrowed from Dwarka Dass Library. The library had the latest books on the history of revolutionary movements in Italy, Russia, Ireland and China. Their primary interests were politics and economics but they also shared a common interest in the aesthetic aspects of life. They found time to pursue music and art, the only digression from their discussions on revolution and revolutionaries.

One day, Bhagat Singh told Durga Devi how he vehemently differed with Sukhdev over their views regarding Cimourdain, a character in *Ninety Three*, a novel by Victor Hugo. Sukhdev condemned Cimourdain for committing suicide. He could not overcome the pangs of conscience for having sentenced Guviano, his comrade, to death because he was the person with whom he had shared his dreams. Sukhdev said Cimourdain surrendered himself to sentimentalism, which did not behove a revolutionary.

But Bhagat Singh defended Cimourdain's action on the ground that he did his duty towards the revolutionary cause when he sentenced Guviano to death. The reason why Cimourdain committed suicide, Bhagat Singh argued, was because of the love he had for Guviano. He could not reconcile the two—his love for his friend and his duty as a judge. For Bhagat Singh, matters of the heart were important. A revolutionary could not be devoid of human feelings, which, in fact, is what made him different from a terrorist. To him, human emotions mattered greatly for this is what saved the radicals from senseless violence. Bhagat Singh did not want the revolutionaries to be devoid of emotion or sentiment and turn into wooden gods.

Bhagat Singh's humane approach betrayed romanticism, Sukhdev would say. It made a revolutionary soft and sentimental. How different were the two? One never turned his back against mercy. The other considered it a hindrance in the way of the elimination of the enemy. When engaged in a fight, Bhagat Singh favoured as little damage as possible. Sukhdev knew no limits. Bhagat Singh told Durga Devi that with the passage of time, the differences in their approach had become increasingly pronounced. Still he would go by Sukhdev's wishes.

Bhagat Singh was now a lot more relaxed. He found an attentive listener in Durga Devi. He wanted to share with her every thought, every emotion. She was surprised because she had known him as a revolutionary, led by his head, not by his heart.

India represented a quest for fulfillment, Bhagat Singh told her. Many outsiders thought the country was lost in troubles and turbulence. But they missed the point. Its capacity to face problems was tremendous. Such a nation could never be defeated. It could withstand any vicissitudes. He recited a verse by Swami Ramatirtha:

> *Ham rukhe tukade khayenge. Bharat par ware jayenge*
> *Ham sukhe channe chabayenge, Bharat ki baat banayenge.*
> *Ham nange umar bitayenge, Bharat par jaan mitayenge.*

(We shall subsist on crumbs, but sacrifice ourselves for Bharat,
We shall live on parched gram, but shall live for Bharat.
We shall go naked our whole lives, but offer our lives to Bharat.)

Bhagat Singh narrated how Ramatirtha often wept while seeing the setting sun in America: "Now you are rising in my beloved country. Drop my tears like dew drops over the beautiful waterfed fields of India."

As he admired Ramatirtha from Punjab, Bhagat Singh also praised Swami Vivekananda from Bengal. He felt proud that both men earned fame for propagating the glory of Indian metaphysics abroad. He woefully noted that Vivekananda's mission became a permanent institution in Bengal, while Ramatirtha did not have even a memorial in Punjab.

Both of them believed in the assertion of man but not in selfishness. Indeed, real progress, Bhagat Singh felt, would come only when an opportunity was given to every individual to develop for the good of the whole community. The touchstone should be how far any political, social or economic theory enabled the individual to rise above his petty self and think in terms of the good of all.

How close, Bhagat Singh thought, he had come to Durga Devi in the last two days. At first he had known her only as Bhagwati Charan's wife and then as a comrade who presided over the meeting where they took the decision to kill Scott, and then as a person who helped him escape from the jaws of death. Now the relationship seemed more personal. It elated him.

Bhagat Singh was drowned in thoughts when Durga Devi told him that they were approaching Calcutta. Indeed, the train was slowing down. The greenery of the lush countryside was rapidly devoured by concrete buildings. A maze of railway lines criss-crossed and ran along the train tracks.

The platform was full of memsahibs and sahibs, authoritative in their behaviour and loud in their conversation. There was no evidence of the panic which Bhagat Singh imagined would engulf them once they learnt of Saunders' murder.

Buggy-type cars were parked at the edge of the platform. There was a retinue of liveried, but barefoot, servants taking out the luggage from the upper class compartments. A small contingent of policemen was present, more to ensure security than to search for anyone in particular.

Bhagat Singh, Durga Devi, her child Sachin, and Rajguru got off the train without drawing any attention. Bhagwati Charan met them at the station. He was curious to know who his brother-in-law was because his wife had no brother. He had suspected that Bhagat Singh might be travelling with her. He had read about the murder of Saunders in *The Statesman*.

Although no longer India's capital, Calcutta still had regal splendour. New Delhi was only the political centre, but Calcutta remained the real centre of social, economic and cultural activities. Its buildings were graceful and park-gates elaborate and varied.

Bhagwati Charan knew that before long the police would be looking for Bhagat Singh. He settled Bhagat Singh at the residence of a rich Marwari friend, Chajju Ram, who lived in Alipore, a posh locality where the sprawling bungalows were admired, but never searched. Both Chajju Ram and his wife, Lakshmi Devi, were great admirers of Bhagat Singh. In fact, all revolutionaries evoked awe in the couple: how a handful of them fearlessly defied the mighty white men!

Bhagat Singh was depressed to see rickshaws being pulled by men, a start reminder of the economic exploitation of the country. He enjoyed flitting in and out of tram cars. The Victoria Memorial, although hewn in marble, could not match the beauty of the Taj Mahal at Agra. The memorial in Calcutta was as stern and cold as British rule.

He liked Bengal's gregarious, cosmopolitan and aristocratic atmosphere. There was music and art in the air. But he felt that there was a sense of superiority among the city's people. He was yet to find the best among them. Even the revolutionaries had cooled down. Rash Behari Bose was still there but he was more popular in Punjab than in Bengal.

Bhagat Singh recalled how he nearly came to Calcutta instead of Kanpur, when he ran away from his home. Despite the immense popularity of revolutionaries like Aurobindo Ghosh and Barindra Kumar, the Bengali youth had remained distant. Viceroy Lord Curzon's proposal to partition Bengal had led to a widespread agitation. But the stir had left no mark on the people. In fact, the Bengal revolutionaries, when he met them, thought that the youthful Bhagat Singh was the person who could rekindle the flame. Batukeshwar Dutt taught him Bengali.

Bhagat Singh adopted in Calcutta a new name, Hari. He also wore a dhoti and shawl like the Bengalis. He attended the session of the Indian National Congress in the city but felt disgusted. The goal to be projected before the country was complete independence and a total severance of ties with the British. Congress leaders were still debating the demand for Dominion Status, which gave London the final say. Power with trammels was no power. How could India feel free if it were to remain within the British Empire as a dominion? And he did not hear a word about radical changes in the country.

The Congress, he found, was still in the hands of the middle class. It wanted to secure rights for the rich by putting pressure on the government. As far as the millions of workers and farmers were concerned, they figured nowhere in the reckoning of the Congress. "If we want to fight for the country's independence, workers, farmers and the common man will have to be brought to the fore." Bhagat Singh had no doubt about it. But, he felt, the Congress leaders did not want to broaden the mass base of the party's membership because they were afraid of revolution. The responsibility had fallen on the shoulders of the revolutionaries to liberate the workers and farmers, not only from the yoke of foreign rule but also from the control of landlords and the rich.

The Congress session bored him. He went straight to a movie hall. To his delight, *Uncle Tom's Cabin* was being screened. He admired Abraham Lincoln, who fought a civil war but did not allow the southern states of America to secede from the northern states over the troublesome issue regarding the abolition of slavery. Lajpat Rai's words of Hindu and Muslim India came to his mind. He hoped it would never come to that. If it ever did, it would be the end of socialist ideology. The British policy of divide and rule would leave behind a bitter legacy and a divided nation, Bhagat Singh feared.

While in Calcutta, he met revolutionaries such as Prafulla Ganguli, Jyotish Ghosh, Trailokyanath Chakraborti, Phonindra Nath Ghosh and Jatindra Nath Das. Most of the revolutionaries of Bengal were in the city at that time. They had discarded what they termed as 'anarchism', or the path of the bomb and the gun. They felt it was possible to fight for socialism through the mobilisation of the masses. They did not believe that the Kakori train dacoity or Saunders' killing had taken the country nearer to the goal of full independence, much less to revolutionary conditions.

The Bengal revolutionaries had, however, come a long way. Their predecessors approached people in the name of religion. The Anushilan Samiti, which was formed in Calcutta in 1894, had divided revolutionaries into two categories: those who believed in religion and those who did not. Most revolutionaries of Bengal at that time were influenced by Bankim Chandra Chatterjee and Vivekananda. Samiti members had to read Hindu scriptures, especially the Gita. Songs and slogans based on Hindu myths inspired Bengal's revolutionaries in the early twentieth century?

The Chapekar brothers, who were among the first revolutionaries to shoot a Briton—Rand, for his tyrannical rule in Poona during the plague—drew their inspiration from Hindu rites and rituals. They were openly anti-Muslim. Vir Savarkar, who spent years in the Andaman cellular jail, was also a revolutionary of the same brand, staunchly anti-British but fanatically pro-Hindu. Bhagat Singh knew all that. He felt happy that the Punjab revolutionaries were made of different stuff, secular to the core.

The Hindu Sanrakshani Samiti (Society for the Protection of Hindus), started by the Chapekar brothers of Maharashtra, did not change. But Bengal's Anushilan Samiti did. In a declaration in 1902, it said: "Humanity cannot progress under inequalities. We shall have to bring equality amongst all men by abolishing inequality of wealth, social inequality, communal inequality and regional inequality. This can be achieved only through a national government." The Bengal revolutionaries had given up their religious fundamentalism when Bhagat Singh met them.

Chakraborti advised him to build a volunteer corps of 5,000 young men on the pattern of the corps the Congress had decided to raise. He found them secular. They enunciated for the first time the belief that religion and politics should not be mixed. Forming a corps was not a new suggestion. Bhagat Singh and his comrades had constituted in April 1925 the Naujawan Bharat Sabha, a platform for the youth. Its manifesto, written by Bhagwati Charan, exhorted the youth to think independently, calmly and patiently and urged them to adopt India's independence as the sole purpose of their lives.

The manifesto said: "Was it not the young Russians who sacrificed their lives for Russia's emancipation?" Their example was compared with that of Indians. There was a warning for the youth. "A branch of a *peepal* tree is cut and religious feelings of the Hindus are injured. A corner of a paper, *tazia* of the idol-breaker Mohammedans is broken, and 'Allah' gets enraged, who cannot be satisfied with anything less than the blood of the infidel Hindus. Man ought to be given more importance than animals and, yet, here in India, they break each other's heads in the name of 'sacred animals'."

Before enrolment, every member of the Sabha had to sign a pledge that he or she would place the interest of the country above that of the community. *Halal* and *Jhatka* meat was cooked together and eaten by Hindus, Muslims and Sikhs.

Bhagat Singh admitted that the Naujawan Bharat Sabha had not yet caught the imagination of the youth. But he believed that all great national movements began with unknown men without much influence. Except for faith and determination, nothing else counted, neither time nor difficulties.

Bhagat Singh recalled Mazzini's words: "Let the boat of life weigh anchor another time. Let it set sail in the Great Ocean." Professor Jai Chand Vidyalankar, who had initiated Bhagat Singh into revolutionary work at National College in Lahore was in Calcutta. He took him to Professor Jyotish Ghosh, a member of the Calcutta Revolutionary Party. Through him Bhagat Singh met many other revolutionaries who had spent the best years of their lives in jail.

Trailokyanath Chakraborti, who had been in prison for 30 years, impressed Bhagat Singh the most. Chakraborti too was struck by Bhagat Singh's revolutionary zeal. But neither Chakraborti nor any other Bengali revolutionary had any faith in the methods that Bhagat Singh and his comrades followed in Punjab and U.P. The killing of individuals, Bhagat Singh argued, was a step meant to harness the enthusiasm of the youth. It was the means, not the end. The end was revolution, in which both Bengal and Punjab concurred. He wanted bombs, and the know-how to manufacture them. Chakraborti believed in Bhagat Singh's integrity and honesty and gave him revolvers and cartridges, although he had said 'no' initially.

In Calcutta Bhagat Singh also met Jatindra Nath Das, a staunch revolutionary who played an important role in giving impetus to the activities of the HSRA. Both men immediately struck a rapport. Das did not, however, agree to teach bomb-making to Bhagat Singh. His party had abandoned "acts of individual terrorism", as he put it, and he, for one, refused to violate the party discipline.

However, Das changed his mind when told by another revolutionary that the killing of top British officials would instil a sense of bravery in the youth and make them participate in revolutionary activities. He noted that panic had already gripped the British after some killings. The old placid situation had undergone a sea-change.

If nothing else, Bhagat Singh's visit to Calcutta revived the sagging spirits of the revolutionaries in Bengal. Once again, there were animated discussions on how to bring about a change in the social structure. The Russian revolution of 1917 had enthused all of them. It had taken time to percolate ideas. But it was increasingly becoming popular to be progressive and a sympathiser of the poor.

Democracy was theoretically a system of political and legal equality. But in concrete and practical terms, it was inadequate. There could be no equality in politics and before the law as long as there were glaring economic inequalities. So long as the ruling class controlled jobs and the press and the schools of the country and all organs of public opinion; so long as it monopolised all trained public functionaries and disposed of unlimited funds to influence elections; so long as laws were made by the ruling class; so long as lawyers, who were private practitioners, sold their expertise to the highest bidder and litigation was exclusive and costly, there would be only nominal equality before the law. So the revolutionaries believed and talked.

The British felt concerned. Sir David Petrie, Director of Criminal Intelligence, warned London about the 'Bolshevik menace'. In a report, he said: "The Bolsheviks are convinced that in the British Empire the most vulnerable point is India... and they cherish it as an article of faith that till India is liberated, Russia will not be rid of the menace of England". Sir James Crerar, then Home Member of the Governor-General's Executive Council, said that India was "getting contaminated by the doctrine and practice of communism".

Confident that some Bengali revolutionaries would step forward to teach the Punjabi revolutionaries how to manufacture the bomb, Bhagat Singh left for Agra in UP. This was to be a new centre for the activities of the revolutionaries.

Three

Bhagat Singh and his two comrades rented two houses at Hing Ki Mandi in Agra. The nearby Jhansi forests were an ideal place to test the bomb. All the revolutionaries, who escaped from Punjab after Saunders' killing, gathered there. Like the building at Mozang Road in Lahore, the Agra houses came to be both their refuge and a rendezvous. Azad, Bhagat Singh, Rajguru and Sukhdev were all present. Along with Jatindra Nath Das, Lalit Mukherji, another revolutionary from Bengal, joined them to train them in bomb-making.

It was a spartan life at Agra. They did not have enough cots to sleep on, not enough utensils to cook and not enough money to buy food. There were days when a few of them would either skip an afternoon meal or dinner in order to manage within their skimpy resources.

Azad, who managed the finances, tapped many important people for money. Motilal Nehru and Purshottam Das Tandon, senior UP Congress leaders, were regular contributors. Some Indian officials sent money through messengers. Once Azad was surprised to get a bearer cheque from Bengal's Advocate General. He encashed it immediately so as not to leave any trace of his whereabouts.

Austerity was a trait the revolutionaries had acquired over a long period. Hardship did not matter. They had opted for such a life, away from their homes and their dear ones. It was not for honour, fame or self-applause, but for the glory of the cause.

The revolutionaries would debate about everything on earth, whether it was economic, political or social. They believed that the state was not really an end in itself and man was not there for the sake of law or the state, but that the state and law existed for man. The touchstone should be how far any political or social theory enabled man to rise above his petty self and think in terms of the good of all.

It was like a study circle which met and discussed things practically everyday. Their long debates made the atmosphere heavy. To bring some relief, Rajguru one day tore a picture of a girl in a bathing suit from a magazine and pinned it on the wall. When Azad returned, he was furious to see the picture and tore it to pieces. He said the revolutionaries could not indulge in the luxury of entertainment. Theirs was a long and dreary life. Rajguru was not present to face Azad's wrath. But when he returned, he noticed the absence of the picture. Before Rajguru could ask, Azad admitted he had ripped the photograph off their wall. To add to Rajguru's hurt, Azad said that he would destroy anything beautiful, even the Taj Mahal.

"We are out to make the world beautiful. How can he talk like this?" Rajguru remarked. But Azad was talking only in anger. Lack of action—and progress—was telling on the revolutionaries. As tempers cooled, Azad apologised for his remark and said he was not against beauty but they could not afford to lose their focus.

The incident made the study circle more serious and businesslike. Bhagat Singh would go to a local library in the morning and share with his colleagues in the afternoon the information he culled from the books. One day he said that despite his best efforts, he could not find any revolutionary party that had clear ideas about what it was fighting for.

The only exception, he said, was the *Ghadar* (rebellion) party which, having been inspired by the US form of government, clearly stated that it wanted to replace the existing system by a Republican form of government. All other parties, Bhagat Singh said, consisted of men who had one idea: to fight against alien rulers. It was laudable but could not be termed a revolutionary idea.

"We must make it clear that revolution does not mean an upheaval," said Bhagat Singh. "Revolution necessarily implies the programme of systematic reconstruction of society on a new and better adopted basis, often necessitating complete destruction of the existing state of affairs. It was one of the illusions of each generation that the social institutions in which it lived were natural and permanent. Yet for countless years social institutions had been superceded by others adopted to temporary needs."

The *Ghadar* party was one of his inspirations. It was the first militant group, which had tried to liberate India by force, something he and his comrades were trying to do. The party was constituted by Indians living in Canada and the US in 1913 to wage war against the British raj. The party's objective was: "What is our name? *Ghadar.* What is our work? *Ghadar.* Where will *Ghadar* break out? In India. The time will soon come when rifles and blood will take the place of pen and ink."

The party was secular, an idea that was dear to Bhagat Singh's heart. One of the booklets which the *Ghadar* party issued, had the following poem:

> No Pundits or Mullahs do we need
> No prayers or litanies we need recite
> These will only scuttle our boat
> Draw the sword: this time to fight.
> Though Hindus, Mussalmans and Sikhs we be,
> Sons of Bharat are we still
> Put aside your arguments for another day
> Call of the hour is to kill.
> While we were all sunk in stupor
> The foreigners took over our government
> In pointless disputes we got involved
> Like quarrelsome whores our time we spent
> Though born we were in one land
> By caste we became high and low
> These foolish factions we did create
> And seeds of discord ourselves did sow.
> Some worship the cow; others, swine abhor,
> The white man eats them at every place;
> Forget you are Hindu, forget you are Mussalman,
> Pledge yourselves to your land and race.

At a time when Maharashtra and Bengal were in the grip of Hindu revivalism—the first resounded with the call of Shivaji and the second with the sentiments of Kali, the goddess of destruction—the *Ghadar* party sustained its faith in secularism. Muslims had been kept away from the uprisings. Nationalist leader Tilak called them *mlechhas* (unclean).

The Sikhs were the backbone of the *Ghadar* party. Gurmukhi was its language and the gurudwara its meeting venue. The party brought Sikhs back into the political mainstream and washed away a stigma on the community for having supported the British in the first national uprising in 1857.

The *Ghadar* party's rebellion started when its party leader
Gurdit Singh, who was from Amritsar, chartered the *Komagata
Maru*, a Japanese merchant ship to Canada in 1914. It carried 376
Indians, mostly Sikhs, to Canada. There was no bar against Indian
immigrants to that country at that time.

When the ship arrived in Canadian waters, it was cordoned off
and the passengers were told that they did not have the right to
land. Gurdit Singh was pressurised to pay charter dues at one go.
He said he would do so after selling its cargo but the ship was not
allowed to unload its cargo.

Indians in Vancouver agitated for the release of the ship. The
most prominent among them was Hussain Rahim, a lawyer. Some
Canadians also joined them. Fitzgerald, a socialist, gave a call
which Bhagat Singh repeated to his comrades: "Get up and arm
yourselves and fight to regain liberty. Inspire your countrymen to
return and sweep all the whites from India."

The Viceroy at New Delhi showed no sympathy with the stranded
passengers. Nor did he intervene to end their nightmare. Eventually,
Canadian guns forced the *Komagata Maru* to return after about two
months. It found no port on the way to Calcutta to berth.

Mewa Singh, an unknown local priest, avenged the humiliation
by shooting William Hopkinson dead in the Vancouver court
where he was waiting to denounce the philosophy which the
Ghadar party was trying to expound. Before Mewa Singh was
executed, he issued a statement: "My religion does not teach me to
bear enmity towards anybody, no matter what class, creed or order
he belongs to. Nor had I any enmity with Hopkinson."

Ultimately, the *Komagata Maru* docked at the Hooghly's Budge
Budge Harbour. The police searched the ship but found no arms.
The passengers were herded in a train and sent to Punjab. Some of
them insisted on depositing a copy of the *Granth Sahib* at a Calcutta
gurudwara. The police opened fire on the procession carrying the
holy book from the harbour and killed 18 people. Over 200 of them
were put in jail.

The *Komagata Maru* incident provided the spark that lit the fire
of defiance among Indians abroad. The *Ghadar*, the party's organ,
wrote relentlessly to exhort people to revolt. Several thousand men
living abroad caught the earliest boat to India.

The *Portland Telegram* gave a communal angle to the report:

HINDUS GO HOME TO FIGHT REVOLUTION

Astoria (Oregon) August 7: "Every train and boat for the south carries large numbers of Hindus from this city and if the exodus keeps up much longer, Astoria will be entirely deserted by the East Indians. The majority of the Hindus employed at Hammond Hills have gone and the balance are preparing to depart in the immediate future. It is alleged that the men are returning to India by way of San Francisco, where it is said, a vessel had been chartered to aid in a revolution which is expected to break out in India as a result of England being occupied in the general European war. It is said that a Japanese steamer will carry the Hindus to their native land."

The *Ghadar* party was leaderless at that time. Secretary General Hardayal had escaped to Switzerland after having been denounced 'an anarchist' in San Francisco. Sohan Singh Bhakna and Kartar Singh, two other leaders, had reached India. Ram Chandra, a nominee of Hardayal, headed the *Ghadar* party. He told all Indians to assemble at Moga in Punjab. "Your duty is clear. Go to India. Stir up rebellion in every corner of the country. Rob the wealthy and show mercy to the poor. In this way gain universal sympathy. Arms will be provided to you on arrival in India. Failing this, you must ransack the police stations for rifles. Obey without hesitation the commands of your leaders."

Another ship, the *Korea*, carried some Indians, who were arrested as soon as the boat reached Calcutta. A few who could evade the police reached Moga. But they did not get arms, although they waited for days. They had no recourse except to disperse to their villages.

People, coming from Hong Kong, China, Japan, Borneo and the Philippines, made contacts with the Indian troops serving in those areas. None of them responded except the 26th Punjabi Regiment at Singapore. The British crushed the rebellion ruthlessly.

On the other hand, most *Ghadarites*, coming through the northern ports, were arrested. But many, travelling through the southern parts, reached Punjab—nearly 1,000 of them. The government passed on March 19, 1915, the Defence of India Act, which authorised the administration "to empower any civil or military authority to prohibit the entry or residence in any area, of a person, suspected to be acting in a manner prejudicial to the public safety, or to direct the residence of such person in any specified area".

They suffered because there was no programme, no strategy. Alas, there was no revolutionary leader, Bhagat Singh said, to make use of the *Ghadarites*. They found the people in Punjab uncooperative. There was no agitation against the British, although World War I, which had started, provided the best opportunity. Gandhi had, instead, volunteered for medical service in the military. Radicals like Tilak too did not want to stall the war efforts. The *Ghadarites* got no response. They were treated as unwanted people. The police, without any inhibition, arrested and harassed them. Some of them were even killed.

The judicial report on the Budge Budge Harbour shooting confirmed the cold reception that the *Ghadarites* got there. "The peasantry saw nothing justifiable in their acts, from whatever patriotic motive they might have been committed. To them, the revolutionaries became murderers and plunderers of honest men... to be resisted by all means possible and captured."

Still, the *Ghadarites* did not give up. They contacted Rash Behari Bose, a revolutionary, who had then shifted the centre of activities from Calcutta to Lahore. His men approached Indian soldiers at several cantonments. The one at Ferozepur was considered the best bet. Bose believed that the soldiers there would rebel and that would spark off a popular uprising. He expected Afghanistan to recognise to the revolutionary government which they would establish.

Bose fixed February 21, 1915 as the date for the uprising. The 23rd Cavalry at Lahore and subsequently other cantonment troops were to shoot British officers, capture arsenal and distribute rifles among the revolutionaries. The *Ghadarites* established factories at Amritsar and Jhabal, near Ludhiana, to manufacture bombs. They were trained to derail trains and cut telegraph lines. Posters about the *Ilan-e-Jung* (declaration of war) were cyclostyled and kept ready for distribution.

But one of the *Ghadarites*, Mula Singh, was arrested accidentally and he told the police everything. Bose advanced the date to February 19. The regiments he had named were disarmed. Many *Ghadarites* were picked up and executed. Some others waited elsewhere for the troops to join them. They too were arrested by the police. Bose managed to escape.

As many as 249 *Ghadarites* were tried. Forty-two were sentenced to death, 114 sent to the Andamans and 93 sentenced to varying terms of imprisonment. The 23rd Cavalry was transferred to Assam but the bombs that exploded from their luggage gave them away. Twelve of them were hanged and six sentenced to life imprisonment.

Thus the *Ghadar* movement was crushed. But it gave birth to the radical Akali movement. The Babbars, Akali terrorists, were born out of the *Ghadar* movement. They killed many Britons to avenge the death of the *Ghadarites*. Some of them, after serving their sentence, returned to Punjab to revive the rebellion against the British. A few left wing political movements took shape. *Kirti* was one of them.

Bhagat Singh traced all this for his comrades to impress upon them that death was something routine in revolution. There was no doubt about the bravery of the *Ghadarites*, or the sacrifices they had made. Many others had followed their example and many more would. How far had they succeeded?

Increasingly, Bhagat Singh and his comrades asked themselves the same questions: Were they achieving what they had left their homes for? Was the country closer to revolution because of their efforts? Should they change their tactics or compromise?

They had no answers. Nor did they have any illusions. They were sure that however limited their success, there was no doubting the goal. Subjection to foreign rule was one of the most potent reasons for the decay of the nation. Any country that rose against its oppressors was bound to fail in the beginning. It could gain partial reforms during its struggle. But it was only in the last stage—having organised all the forces and resources of the nation—that it could possibly strike the final blow to shatter the foreign government.

Nonetheless, Bhagat Singh and his comrades wondered whether their tactics had yielded the results they had envisaged. The bomb might be necessary at times to arouse attention. But they also had to convince people through argument and personal example that theirs was the best way to release the common man from the slavery of foreigners.

The government machinery was a weapon in the hands of the ruling class to safeguard its interests. "We want to snatch and handle it to utilise it for the consummation of our ideal, that is, social reconstruction." But then, Bhagat Singh said: "We have to educate the masses to create a favourable atmosphere for our social programmes."

The revolutionaries had a feeling that the temper of the country was becoming more liberal. Nehru too noted the gentle breeze of socialism that was blowing across the country. Congress workers were borrowing books by Bryce on democracy and Mazzini on revolution. The British found from intelligence reports that the influence of the revolutionaries was spreading among workers, students and the youth. Trade union activities had gathered strength. Even some Indian officials were suspected of sympathising with the revolutionaries.

Bhagat Singh and his comrades discussed the fallout of the Saunders killing at the Agra house. They realised that it had not produced the desired results. There had been no exodus of the British as they had imagined. Only a few had sent their wives back to England. Initial panic had given place to the belief among the British that repression would teach the rebellious a lesson. The Congress or Gandhi posed no problem to them. The revolutionaries did. That was the time when the British decided to bring two bills before the Central Assembly to curb political and labour activities and counter the revolutionaries' appeal.

Both bills were meant to smother resistance to British rule. The first bill, the Public Safety Bill, was designed to empower the government to detain anyone without trial. The second, the Trade Disputes Bill, was meant to deter labour unions from organising strikes, particularly in Bombay, where mill-owners had been forced to increase wages.

At their headquarters in Agra, the revolutionaries sat for hours debating the effect of the two bills on the country and their movement. They considered the Assembly a worthless institution. They believed it demonstrated to the world the humiliation and helplessness of Indians and gave credibility to the domination of an irresponsible and autocratic rule. Still the Assembly mattered because it put an official stamp on the illegitimate governance.

They wondered if it was a forum they could use to make the point that the bills would make British tyranny more tyrannical? Was the Assembly the right place to raise their protest? The bills were, in fact, meant to give a clear message to the revolutionaries to get prepared for more suppression and punishment. Should they respond to the challenge? It meant coming out in the open to test their own popularity and that of the HSRA.

Although they were making some headway, they felt handicapped because their work, by its very nature, was secretive. The bills would only throttle them further. How their message should reach the public was the topic before them during the discussions in the Agra houses. Saunders' killing had brought them into national prominence. But that was more than a year ago. What should they do to re-focus the spotlight on themselves and their message? Another killing of a British official? Would it help? Already, there was a strong belief that public mobilisation was the real thing, not an occasional bomb explosion or killing.

They were conscious that any protest outside the Assembly would land them in trouble. They would be arrested and jailed straightaway. They then thought they could instead use the Assembly hall for the propagation of their message. Some peaceful way to register their presence and protest was necessary. It would also defeat the malicious propaganda by the British that they were "a bunch of killers". The government had deliberately given them a bad name. They had to repudiate it.

A formal meeting of the HSRA was called to decide on the next step. Bhagat Singh, as usual, was the first to speak. He said: "The British are out to loot and kill us, without even allowing us to raise our voice. More repressive laws will follow. Slaves as we are, we will have no scope even to protest." He already had consulted Sukhdev in Lahore on the mode of voicing their opposition. Tara Chand, a comrade from UP, saw Bhagat Singh's point. He said: "There is no other way except to open the eyes and ears of the Assembly members, particularly the Indians." Azad intervened to ask: "How?" The central idea was to express resentment against the bills.

They finally decided that two comrades from among them would hurl bombs from the public gallery at the treasury benches in the Central Assembly Hall, taking care not to hurt anyone. The explosion was sure to start a debate on why the two young men had chosen the secure environs of the Assembly to risk their lives. It would make people think. People would realise how the revolutionaries had braved dangers to register their protest against the jungle raj that the British had come to represent in the country.

Two people, B.K. Dutt and Ram Saran Das, were nominated for the task. The latter, convicted in 1915, had recently returned from the Andamans after serving a sentence. Following his release, he had contacted Bhagat Singh and had become an activist in the HSRA.

Das had authored a book, *Dreamland,* to which Bhagat Singh had written an introduction. They were poles apart in their views. Still they were close. Bhagat Singh wrote: "His interpretation of the universe is ideological and metaphysical, while I am a materialist and my interpretation of the phenomenon would be casual. Nevertheless, it is by no means out of place or out of date. The general ideas that are prevailing in our country, are more in accordance with those expressed by him. To fight that depressing mood, he resorted to prayers."

"The whole of the beginning of the book," Bhagat Singh wrote, "is devoted to God. His praise, His definition, belief in God is the outcome of mysticism which is the natural consequence of depression. That this world is *maya* or *mithya,* dream or fiction, is clear mysticism which has been originated and developed by Hindu sages, such as Sankaracharya and others. But in the materialist philosophy this mode of thinking has got absolutely no place. This mysticism of the author is by no means ignoble or deplorable. It has its own beauty and charm."

Bhagat Singh wished he had been selected to throw the bomb. He would have used the courtroom to declare that the purpose of the explosion was to warn the British that the unrest of the people was increasing and that things could take a serious turn if they were not tackled in time.

Bhagat Singh's suggestion to go in place of Das elicited one response: he could be considered if he could escape after throwing the bomb, as he had done after killing Saunders. But he rejected the idea.

He said that the time had come to prepare for a wordy duel. Nothing had ever remained of any revolution but what was ripe in the conscience of the masses. Words could do that. They must be told. The rulers must be put in the dock. The courts should be used as a forum to propagate revolutionary patriotic ideas and to rekindle fervour for the country's freedom. The public must know the motive of the revolutionaries.

If the motive was set aside, said Bhagat Singh. "Jesus Christ will appear to be a man responsible for creating disturbances, breaking peace and preaching revolt and will be considered to be a dangerous personality in the language of the law. But we worship him."

R.H. Tawney's *The Acquisitive Society* was the most recent book Bhagat Singh had read. *The Acquisitive Society*, he said, "was a reality". The reason why people from the Tawney age adopted the socialist creed was the degrading economic and moral conditions under which so many people lived at that time. He underlined the contradiction between political freedom and economic dependence and underscored the necessity of freedom for economic improvement . The history of all societies, Bhagat Singh said, was the history of class struggles. It was a fight between those "who do not work" and "those who do". It had been caused not by subversion or conspiracies and astute political leaders, but by the same inexorable social laws that destroyed previous systems like feudalism in Europe.

What Bhagat Singh was trying to convey was that he would be the best exponent of their philosophy. But Azad, who was presiding over the meeting, ruled him out. He did not want to expose him to the danger which loomed large. He was aware that Bhagat Singh was wanted by the Punjab police. Once they laid their hands on him, they would take him to court. The trial was sure to end in his conviction and hanging.

One point which generated some heat following the selection of the team was whether Dutt and Ram Saran should be rescued after they had thrown the bombs. Azad recalled how he had led his comrades to safety after the Saunders murder. But then the aim was different. This time the idea was to surrender so that people could see that the revolutionaries had sacrificed themselves to register their protest against the oppressive measures the British were determined to enact. Dutt and Ram Saran would not try to escape but would use the forum of the court to explain themselves and their concept of revolution.

When Sukhdev came to know that Bhagat Singh was not in the team, he was greatly upset. He took up the matter with Azad. If anyone among them could put across the party's point of view cogently and lucidly and defend the use of violence, it was Bhagat Singh, Sukhdev argued. "We are sick of the stigma of violence attached to us. We are neither killers, nor terrorists. We want the country and the world to know about our faith in revolution." Bhagat Singh had the name, the background and the commitment to explain their aspirations, Sukhdev said.

Bhagat Singh too was tired of violence being associated with them. Gandhi's description of "irresponsible young men" irritated him. He recalled how Lenin once said to Gorky that he could not bear music because it upset his whole nervous system and made him feel like patting the head of the artists. "But," he added, "this is not the time to pat the heads. The hands should descend now to smash the skulls, though our ultimate aim is the elimination of all sorts of violence."

This was how the revolutionaries felt when they had to use guns or bombs. It was a necessity when the action was justified. Had Gandhi ever sat around the evening fire with a peasant and tried to know what he thought? Had he spent a single evening in the company of a factory labourer and shared with him his views? The revolutionaries knew what the masses thought. The day was not far off when they would attract thousands "to work the will of the revolution". So they believed.

When they were building their movement through the Naujawan Bharat Sabha in Punjab and the HSRA, they were aiming at two things. One was to frighten or eliminate the oppressive British officials. The second, more important, was to organise a mass movement of workers, peasants, students and youth. However limited in extent their two-pronged strategy was, they believed they had accelerated the pace of the freedom struggle and drawn people closer to idealism and ideology.

Bhagat Singh said: "There are times when the blow of the enemy has to be immediately counteracted by armed actions to inspire confidence among the masses." It might have led to the belief that their focus was on violence. But the real purpose was to popularise the ideas of socialism, a state without exploitation, not of force.

The court trial would help them make it clear that their philosophy was not violence in general, but violence against the British in particular. They hoped to evoke a public debate on how they had tried to awaken people to the ills of foreign rule, which had aggravated the plight of slum dwellers in industrial areas and villagers living in worn-out cottages or out in the open. They wanted people to rebel, a prerequisite of revolution.

Sukhdev chided Bhagat Singh for not joining the team lest he should be jailed. This was the unkindest cut. Sukhdev compared Bhagat Singh with Bhai Parmanand, a revolutionary who later became a staunch Hindu leader. The reference was to an

observation made by the Lahore High Court in Parmanand's case:
"Although the brain and spirit behind the party, he was a coward
at heart. He sent others to the stake, himself managing to remain
in the background."

"You are insulting me," Bhagat Singh told Sukhdev.

"I am doing my duty towards a friend," said Sukhdev.

Sukhdev did not stop at that. He said: "You would be of no use
to revolution because you are now in the grip of a woman." His
reference was to Durga Devi who had helped Bhagat Singh elude
the police and escape from Lahore after the Saunders murder.

Bhagat Singh kept quiet at that time. Subsequently, he replied
to Sukhdev through an emotional letter. He did not admit whether
he was in love or not, but he did say that love was not incompatible
with the life of a revolutionary. He, however, added that he could
renounce all at the time of need and "that is the real sacrifice".

He gave the example of Mazzini who wrote that after the utter
failure and crushing defeat at the first uprising he could not bear
the misery. The thought of his dead comrades haunted him. One
letter from the girl he loved saved him from going mad or
committing suicide.

"As regards the moral status of love," Bhagat Singh wrote, "I
may say that it in itself is nothing but passion, not an animal
passion but a human one, and very sweet too. Love in itself can
never be an animal passion. Love always elevates the character of
man. It never lowers him, provided love be love... And I may tell
you that a young man and a young girl can love each other, and
with the aid of their love they can overcome the passions
themselves and can maintain their purity." Bhagat Singh sounded
like Gandhi on celibacy.

The tone of Bhagat Singh's letter suggested he had once been
consumed by the feelings of love. He admitted: "I rebuked the love
of one individual... and that too in the idealistic stage. And even
then, man must have the strongest feelings of love which he may
not confine to one individual and may make it universal."

Bhagat Singh made a dig at Sukhdev: "One thing I may tell you
to mark, we, in spite of all radical ideas that we cherish, have not
been able to do away with the over-idealistic Arya Samajist
conception of morality. We may talk glibly about all the radical
things that can possibly be conceived, but in practical life, we begin
to tremble at the very outset."

The letter showed the softer side of Bhagat Singh. He was a revolutionary but that did not make him a stone devoid of feelings. So long as his feelings did not come in the way of his revolutionary work in any manner, how did it matter whether he was up at night to gaze at the stars or whether he strained his ears to hear the refrain of a sad song in the distance.

Durga Devi, intelligent and articulate, had helped him escape the police. He acted as her husband. True, she was married and had a son. But they had worked together. They had shared moments of triumph and despondency. Was there anything beyond that?

What Sukhdev alleged was not hinted at by anybody else, not even by Azad, who was a father figure to Bhagat Singh. Perhaps Azad too felt that love was not a sordid affair, not to be run down or ridiculed, although he was considered "a dangerous revolutionary", who had a price of 30,000 rupees on his head.

He was aware of what Bhagat Singh was going through. The Assembly hall was the end of his journey. He would be arrested, tried for the murder of Saunders and hanged. Azad and Bhagat Singh were not mere comrades. They had travelled a long way together to give shape to the revolutionary movement. They had dreamt together of an India which would be independent and which would then lead the fight to free the enslaved countries of the world. That world would have a socialist order: from each according to his ability, to each according to his need.

At Bhagat Singh's request, there was yet another meeting of the central committee. Sukhdev did not say anything. But his eyes were red as if he had been crying all night. Bhagat Singh was able to prevail upon the members to nominate him in place of Ram Saran Das. He also put an end to the debate on surrender by saying that nobody should be rescued. He and Dutt would throw bombs from the public gallery and do so in such a manner that nobody would be hurt. Since it was meant to draw attention to what they stood for, they would give themselves up after completing their job.

Dutt had been Bhagat Singh's colleague in a Hindi paper, *Pratap*, of Kanpur. Bhagat Singh had then run away from home to escape his father's admonitions on marriage. In Kanpur, he had met Ganesh Shanker Vidyarthi, editor of *Pratap*, who gave him his first job in journalism in 1923. At his behest, Bhagat Singh had covered communal riots in Delhi. His antipathy to religion had only increased after that. (Vidyarthi himself was later a victim of communal violence. During a riot, he rescued many Muslims from Hindu localities. But when he was leading Hindus to Muslim localities, he was murdered.)

Dutt brought back memories of their Kanpur days. Bhagat Singh recalled how the two would discuss changes in India through revolution. It was Dutt who introduced Bhagat Singh to a song, which they often hummed.

> "*Ek halora idhar se aaye*
> *ek halora udhar se aaye*
> *sara ulat phulat ho gaya*
> *dhuan dhar jagat mein chaye*
> *nash aur satyanash ki dhul*
> *udd chale dhayein bhayein.*"

(One gust of wind came from one side and another from the other. Everything became topsy-turvy and the smoke spread all over the world. Let the destroyers be destroyed and let the dust spread right and left.)

It was in Kanpur that the real revolutionary Bhagat Singh was born. It was here that he got a new name, Balwant, and got associated with many revolutionary organisations, particularly those who knew how to make bombs. Azad met him then. Their liking for each other was spontaneous. Both were revolutionaries to the core. It was in Kanpur where Bhagat Singh learnt the ethos of revolution on the ground. Lahore was at best a laboratory. He still had to test what he had learnt or imbibed.

After Bhagat Singh's nomination to the team, Azad knew that Bhagat Singh's days were numbered. Azad could not bring himself to the point of saying goodbye. But he had no doubt that he would not meet Bhagat Singh as a free man again. How short was the span of a revolutionary's life. He was like a shooting star, glowing for a while and then burning out. He had to be an example inspiring others. Would his sacrifice be the foundation stone for the edifice of the revolution? Would people realise that he could not put up any longer with the lack of respect for Indians?

Even when Lenin triumphed in Russia, it was their humiliation over the defeat in the war that gave Russian forces a purpose to arise to erase the stigma. Lenin only articulated that purpose. His revolutionary work among them was of little help.

Azad told Shiv Verma, another comrade: "In a few days, history will claim them (Bhagat Singh and Dutt) and only a legend would survive through the corridors of time."

Viceroy Irwin scheduled the two bills for discussion on April 8, 1929. The revolutionaries also chose the same day to register their protest. They knew that the British judicial system would never be fair to them after their arrest. They would stage a farce of justice, not real justice.

The revolutionaries were determined to tell the British not to take the country for granted. The attack in the Assembly hall would send shivers through mighty London and make it clear to it that the revolutionaries could reach any place to seek their target.

Two days before they were to throw the bombs, both Bhagat Singh and Dutt got themselves photographed at a shop near Kashmere Gate in Old Delhi. Bhagat Singh was keen on having a photograph of himself as a free man. He had a premonition that he would not come out alive from the task he had undertaken to accomplish.

Even after nine-and-a-half months, the police had failed to find out who had killed Saunders. The Viceroy's telegram to the Secretary of State at that time said: "The investigation in the Saunders murder case is not having much progress." London's reply was that "it is very disappointing to hear that progress of investigation is not so satisfactory".

Four

Away from the sounds and smells of Old Delhi, the new city of New Delhi, imposing and impersonal, had come up with high buildings and vaulted chambers. It was characterised by its distinctive columns and red stone buildings. A British architect from London, Lutyens, had planned the city and guided its construction. One building was the Council House, the Central Legislative Assembly, built by Baker. It was a monumental edifice with the extravagant proportions of corridor space, dubbed by critics as a 'dreary-go-round'.

Both Bhagat Singh and Dutt visited the Assembly on April 6, 1929, two days before the bills were to be introduced. They wanted particularly to see the public gallery overlooking the hall. They had to make sure the bombs they threw did not hurt anyone.

Wearing khaki shirts and shorts they got into the public gallery, unnoticed, a few minutes before the session began on April 8 at 11 a.m. An Indian member of the Assembly gave them passes at the entrance and then disappeared. The gallery was overflowing with visitors. They could see in the distinguished gallery Simon against whose commission they had demonstrated outside the Lahore railway station. Inside the house, they recognised some national leaders—Moti Lal Nehru, Mohammad Ali Jinnah, N.C. Kelkar and M.R. Jayakar.

Their bombs, Bhagat Singh knew, could not stop the bills from becoming acts. The British had their 'yesmen' to put the legal stamp on them. Even otherwise, the Viceroy had extraordinary powers. But they would at least administer a warning that the simmering lava of resentment against the British government and its methods would spew out one day and burn foreign rule. Bhagat Singh recalled the words of Valliant, a French anarchist: "It takes a loud voice to make a deaf hear." The bombs would create enough noise to grab attention.

Bhagat Singh chose the moment carefully. The Trade Disputes Bill, which sought to ban general strikes by industrial workers, had been passed by the Central Legislative Assembly. But the President, Vithalbhai Patel, had not yet given his ruling on the Public Safety Bill* to empower the government to detain suspects without trial.

The first bomb was carefully hurled by Bhagat Singh on the floor. It exploded with a bang. The hall plunged into darkness. There was confusion in the visitors' gallery. Shrieks of ladies rose above the din all around. Yet another bomb was thrown by Dutt, emitting thick black smoke. People in the public gallery ran towards the exit, jamming the passage in panic.

The first bang confused the members in the house. The second one scared them. Many ran for shelter, including the Home Member. Some hid behind the wooden benches in the house. The bombs, deliberately weak in their potency, had been thrown in such a way that they landed at places where nobody was sitting.

The members felt relieved when a sheaf of leaflets came fluttering down from the gallery like a shower of leaves. Then they heard the slogans: "*Inquilab Zindabad*" and "Long Live Proletariat". The leaflets covered parts of the floor and some seats. Bhagat Singh himself had written fhe text and had typed 30 to 40 copies on a party letterhead on a machine which Jaidev Kapur, a party member, bought from a Marwari school drill-master.

The members picked up the leaflets and began to read what was written on them.

Hindustan Socialist Republican Association

Notice

"'It takes a loud voice to make a deaf hear.' With these immortal words uttered on a similar occasion by Valliant, a French anarchist martyr, do we strongly justify this action of ours."·

"Without repeating the humiliating history of the past ten years of the working of the reforms (Montague-Chelmsford Reforms) and without mentioning the insults hurled at the Indian nation through this House—the so-called Indian Parliament—we see this time again, while the people, expecting some more crumbs of reforms

---

*The report of the Select Committee on the bill was put to vote and was defeated by the Chair's casting vote. The Chair said: "Here is an equality of votes—61 against 61. My opinion is that, if any party or individual member seeks to put such an extraordinary measure on the statute book, he must persuade the House and get a majority in his favour."

from the Simon Commission, are ever quarrelling over the
distribution of the expected bones, the Government is thrusting
upon us new repressive measures like those of the Public Safety Bill
and the Trade Disputes Bill, while reserving the Press Sedition Bill
for the next session. The indiscriminate arrests of labour leaders
working in the open field clearly indicate whither the wind blows."

"In these provocative circumstances, the Hindustan Socialist
Republican Association, in all seriousness, realising their full
responsibility, had decided and ordered its army to do this
particular action so that a stop be put to this humiliating farce and
to let the alien bureaucratic exploiters do what they wish but to
make to come before the public eye in their naked form."

"Let the representatives of the people return to their constituencies
and prepare the masses for the coming revolution. And let the
government know that, while protesting against the Public Safety
Bill and the Trade Disputes Bill and the callous murder of Lala
Lajpat Rai on behalf of the helpless Indian masses, we want to
emphasise the lesson often repeated by history that it is easy to kill
individuals but you cannot kill the ideas. Great empires crumbled
but the ideas survived. Bourbons and Czars fell while the
revolution marched ahead triumphantly."

"We are sorry to admit that we who attach so great a sanctity to
human life, we who dream of a glorious future when man will be
enjoying perfect peace and full liberty, have been forced to shed
human blood. But the sacrifice of individuals at the altar of the
great revolution that will bring freedom to all, rendering the
exploitation of man by man impossible, is inevitable."

Long Live Revolution.

Balraj
Commander-In-Chief.

As the members began returning to their seats, they saw two
young men standing in the public gallery. After throwing the
bombs, Bhagat Singh and Dutt did not try to escape in the
confusion that prevailed. Instead they stood there as decided by
their party. They close to be arrested so that they could use the
occasion to explain their reasons. They looked forward to the
opportunity they would get in the court.

Policemen stayed away from them, fearing the two were armed.
They were not and said so to the policemen. Their purpose was

merely to create a bang and open the ears of the rulers, and that they had succeeded in doing.

Bhagat Singh surrendered his automatic pistol, which he had used to pump bullets into Saunders' body. Although he and Dutt assured the authorities that they carried no arms on them the policemen approached them haltingly. The two were then handcuffed and searched. A British officer, who ran away on hearing the explosion, hurriedly came back and supervised the arrest. Both were taken to different police stations, Bhagat Singh to the main one and Dutt to one at Chandni Chowk. The purpose was to question them separately. Both were kept in solitary confinement.

The authorities suspected that the bombings were a sign of things to come. They feared a series of violent incidents would follow the explosion in the Assembly. The press was asked to play down the Assembly incident. Though most versions that appeared in print were abridged, *The Hindustan Times*, New Delhi, managed to give the story a three-deck headline:

Bombs and Pistols create chaos in Assembly; Two Bombs Explode, Pistol Shots Fired

Screaming Women from Ladies' Gallery; Sir Fomanji Dalal Seriously Injured, Two Arrested

Sir George Schuster, Mr. S.C. Gupta and others officials received minor injuries.

The Viceroy came out with a special statement where he conceded that the "two asssailants" had taken care not to kill anyone. He admitted that they could have caused havoc if they had so desired. But he said that their target was the 'institution' of the Central Assembly. Congress member Chaman Lall, reputed to be progressive in his leanings was the first to denounce the revolutionaries. He said the bomb throwing was an act of madness. The revolutionaries treated his observation with contempt.

The government was, however, intrigued by the two revolutionaries giving themselves up so easily. Would they escape from jail? Was it meant to fool the rulers? The British did not want to take any chances. So, even the summons to the two were delivered in jail.

The authorities had a feeling that in Bhagat Singh they had caught a big fish. They believed he was probably the main man behind revolutionary activities in India. They even suspected him to be one of Saunders' killers. The language in the handbills seemed familiar to British intelligence. A senior police officer was sent to Lahore to scrutinise the posters pasted on the city's walls to announce the murder of Saunders.

The typed handbills and handwritten posters had certain common features. Both were on pink paper. Both were issued by the Hindustan Socialist Republican Association, and both had the party's name on top. There were other similarties. Both were signed by Balraj, commander-in-chief. And both began with the word 'Notice' and ended with the slogan, 'Long Live Revolution'.

Even the words used were similar. The last paragraph of the handbills thrown in the Assembly was: "We are sorry to admit that we, who attach so great a sanctity to human life, we, who dream of a glorious future when man will be enjoying perfect peace and full liberty, have been forced to shed human blood. But the sacrifice of individuals at the altar of the great revolution that will bring freedom to all rendering the exploitation of man by man impossible, is inevitable."

The last paragraph of the poster in Lahore read: "Sorry for the bloodshed of a human being; but the sacrifice of individuals at the altar of the Revolution that will bring freedom to all and make the exploitation of man by man impossible, is inevitable."

Suspicion against Bhagat Singh deepened as the inquiry proceeded. He was singled out as the author of the text on the leaflets as well as the poster. Indeed, he was. He had written both in his own hand.

That the case was directed more against him did not worry Bhagat Singh. He had anticipated the direction of the case from the day he replaced Das to throw the bomb. He had been preparing for a public appearance in court since then. He wanted to use the court as a platform to advocate the revolutionaries' point of view and in the process try to rekindle patriotic sentiments. If there was no struggle, there was no progress. People who said they favoured freedom and yet deprecated agitations were like men who wanted the final crop without ploughing the ground.

Bhagat Singh was charged with attempt to murder under section 307 of the Indian Penal Code. Young Asaf Ali, a member of the Congress party, was his lawyer. At the first meeting with him, Bhagat Singh requested him to tell Chaman Lall that they were no lunatics. "We humbly claim to be more serious students of history and the conditions of our country and her aspirations."

The British saw in Bhagat Singh's action a revival of what Madan Lal Dhingra had done in 1909. He had put up no defence for killing Sir William Curzon Wyllie, aide-de-camp to the Secretary of State of India at the Institute of Imperial Studies in London. Dhingra had refused to appear in court to ventilate his feelings against the British. Indeed he issued a statement through *The Daily News* in London.

"I admit, the other day I attempted to shed English blood as a humble revenge for the inhuman hangings and deportations of patriotic Indian youths. In this attempt I have consulted none but my own conscience. I have conspired with none but my own duty."

"I believe that a nation held down by a foreign bayonet is in a perpetual state of war, since open battle is rendered impossible to a disarmed race. I attacked by surprise since guns were denied to me. I drew forth my pistol and fired. As a Hindoo I felt that wrong to my country is an insult to my God. Her cause is the cause of Ram, her service is in the service of Krishna. Poor in wealth and intellect, a son like myself has nothing else to offer to the mother but his own blood and so I have sacrificed the same on her altar. The only lesson required in India at present is to learn how to die and the only way to teach it is by dying ourselves. Therefore, I die and glory in my martyrdom. My only prayer of God is may I be reborn of the same mother and may I re-die in the same sacred cause till the cause is successful and she stands free for the good of humanity and the glory of God—*Bande Mataram.*"

Even after twenty years, the British found the same determination to oust them through bullets and bombs. They compared Bhagat Singh and Dutt to the scores of revolutionaries who had ended up at the gallows. Gandhi was a deeply respected leader. But they found the youth related more to the revolutionaries than to him. People like Bhagat Singh and Dutt were their heroes.

So enthusiastic was their support that the British decided to hold the court in Delhi jail itself (now Maulana Azad Medical College). All roads leading to the jail were guarded. CID men in plainclothes were posted at various points. Everybody entering the court was searched. Even pressmen were not spared.

The Crown was represented by Public Prosecutor Rai Bahadur Suryanarayan. The trial magistrate was a British judge, P.B. Pool. Bhagat Singh's parents were also present in the court.

When Bhagat Singh and Dutt were brought to the court, they raised their clenched fists and shouted: *"Inquilab Zindabad,"*

"Samrajya Murdabad" (down with imperialism). The court recorded the slogans. The magistrate ordered the police to handcuff both of them. They offered no resistance and sat on a bench behind the iron railing which had been put up temporarily.

The prosecution's star witness was Sergeant Terry, who said that a pistol was found on Bhagat Singh when he was arrested in the Assembly. This was not factually correct because Bhagat Singh had himself surrendered the pistol while asking the police to arrest him.

Even the eleven witnesses who said they had seen the two throwing the bombs seemed to have been tutored. The entire incident was so sudden that nobody could have either anticipated or noticed it. Indeed, both Bhagat Singh and Dutt were careful. They had carried the bombs in one pocket and the detonator in another. They walked slowly to make sure that there was no accidental explosion. It was an arduous task: staying apart, and at the same time ensuring that they aroused no suspicion.

The manner in which the prosecution presented its case left Bhagat Singh in no doubt that the British were out to get him. He conveyed his feelings to his father, when he met him and his mother during a lunch break in the presence of police officials.

Bhagat Singh requested the court to allow them newspapers in prison as was the practice for political undertrials. The court turned down the request saying it was not bound to follow any precedent. It treated them as 'criminals'.

When the two were brought to the court on following day, May 8, 1929, they wondered how they would get justice with such a hostile magistrate. As usual they shouted, "Long Live Revolution", "Down with Imperialism" as they entered the court.

Bhagat Singh gave his name when asked. But he replied "none" when questioned about his profession. Asked about his residence, he said: "We are always moving from one place to another."

Judge: "Were you present in the Assembly on the 8th of April, 1929?"

Bhagat Singh: "As far as this case is concerned, I feel no necessity to make a statement at this stage. When I do, I will make the statement."

Judge: "When you arrived in the court, you shouted, 'Long Live the Revolution'. What do you mean by it?"

Asaf Ali objected to the question. The court sustained the objection. Bhagat Singh and Dutt vehemently denied an allegation that they had fired shots in the Assembly. The court then asked Dutt some questions. But he refused to answer any one of them. He thought that Bhagat Singh, as the leader, would attend to all queries.

As if it had already made up its mind, the court framed charges under Section 307 of the Indian Penal Code and Section 3 of the Explosive Substances Act. Bhagat Singh and Dutt were accused of throwing bombs "to kill or cause injuries to the King Majesty's subjects". The court once again asked them to make a statement, but they said, "No".

The magistrate committed both of them to the Sessions Court, presided over by Judge Leonard Middleton. The trial started in the first week of June, 1929. The public prosecutor produced some more witnesses, who too said that they had seen Bhagat Singh and Dutt throwing the bomb in the Assembly hall. The same allegations of firing shots in the air were repeated. The accused once again denied the charge.

Both were specially irked by the allegation of gunshots. It was apparent that the government was not limiting the case to the bombs thrown in the Assembly Chamber. It was introducing extraneous elements in order to find out about their party and the revolutionary programme. This was the stage when they decided to make their statement, which both of them had prepared in jail. Asaf Ali read it out.

The statement did not deny the throwing of the bomb. "It was necessary to awaken England from her dreams," they said. "We dropped the bomb on the floor of the Assembly Chamber to register our protests on behalf of those who had no other means left to give expression to their heartrending agony. Our sole purpose was to make the deaf hear and give the heedless a timely warning."

Bhagat Singh had also a dig at Gandhi. "We have only marked the end of an era of Utopian non-violence of whose futility the rising generation has been convinced beyond the shadow of doubt."

Explaining the concept of violence which the revolutionaries had adopted, Bhagat Singh said: "It was the only effective method of solving the great social problems of the times—the problem of bringing economic and political independence to the workers and peasants, constituting the mass of people." He justified their action after the Trade Disputes Bill was passed. "None whose heart bleeds for them, who have given their life-blood in silence to the building up of the economic structure, could repress the cry which this ruthless blow had wrung out of our hearts."

"We are next to none in our love for humanity. Far from having any malice against any individuals, we hold human life sacred beyond words... The elimination of force at all costs is Utopian, and the new movement which has arisen in the country, and of that dawn we have given a warning, is inspired by the ideals which guided Guru Govind Singh, Shivaji, Kamal Pasha, Riza Khan, Washington, Garibaldi, Lafayette and Lenin. As both the alien government and the Indian public leaders appeared to have shut their eyes to this movement, we felt it is our duty to sound a warning where it could not go unheard... We repeat that we hold human life sacred beyond words, and would sooner lay down our own lives in the service of humanity than injure anyone else... And still we admit having deliberately thrown the bombs into the Assembly Chamber. Facts speak for themselves and our intention would be judged from the result of the action without bringing in Utopian, hypothetical circumstances and presumptions..."

"By revolution," the statement said, "we mean the ultimate establishment of an order of society, which may not be threatened by such breakdown, and in which the sovereignty of the proletariat should be recognised and a world federation should redeem humanity from the bondage of capitalism and misery of imperial wars..."

They said the Viceroy was right when he said that they wanted to hit out at the institution. "Our practical protest was against the institution, which since its birth, has eminently helped to display not only its worthlessness but its far-reaching power for mischief."

Middleton was no better than Pool. He too swallowed the prosecution story. Or was it all pre-determined? The judge accepted the verbal testimony as proof that Bhagat Singh and Dutt had thrown the bombs into the Assembly Chamber. Middleton even said that Bhagat Singh fired from his pistol while scattering the leaflets in the chamber.

The court held both Bhagat Singh and Dutt guilty of "causing explosions of a nature likely to endanger life, unlawfully and maliciously, which constitute an offence punishable under section 3 of the Explosive Substances Act, 1988". They were sentenced to life imprisonment.

In his judgment, Middleton argued that he had no doubt that their acts were "deliberate" and that they had made preparations for "those acts of a complicated nature". He rejected the plea that the bombs were deliberately made weak since the impact of the explosion was so strong, that it shattered one-and-a-half inch thick wood in the Assembly.

The judge did not accept the defence of the accused that they held human life sacred. He said their acts were not justified. "It is probably that what they have done once they might attempt to do again." Middleton said: "Normally, these youths must not be allowed to lead to the infliction of an inadequate punishment." Still he did not want to hang them, the judge said.

Although both Bhagat Singh and Dutt were reluctant to file an appeal, they were persuaded to do so. If the purpose was to use the court as a forum to propagate the message of revolution, then why not exploit every opportunity? The greater the noise, the greater their chances of awakening the masses from their slumber and slavery. The appeal by Bhagat Singh and Dutt was rejected. They were sent to jail for 14 years, the span of life imprisonment.

It was not Bhagat Singh's first introduction to jail. He had been arrested in May 1927 while passing through a garden in Lahore. He did not feel any sensation then. Neither did he experience any excitement. He was first taken into the Railway police lock-up where he was kept for a month. After many days, the police told him that he was "responsible" for throwing a bomb on a crowd during Dussehra which was celebrated a few weeks earlier.

He laughed when they wanted him to turn approver. People with views like his did not throw bombs on the innocent, he said in reply. One fine morning Superintendent of CID Newman came to Bhagat Singh and gave him a long lecture on how the young were led astray by bad elements in society. Bhagat Singh was struck by the sympathetic words he expressed. Newman asked him to confess; otherwise, he said, he would be forced to send Bhagat Singh for trial not only for the 'murders' at Dussehra, but also for the conspiracy to wage war in connection with the Kakori case. The Englishman warned Bhagat Singh that the government had enough evidence to get him convicted and hanged.

But this was not true. They did not have even a shred of evidence against him. Still the judge imposed a hefty bail of 50,000 rupees

before releasing him. Since there was nothing to implicate him, the
remand for bail was also withdrawn later.

The incident had brought Bhagat Singh face to face with realities.
The British would go to any extent to curb a revolt against their
rule. They would frame cases against those who raised their heads
against them. They would imprison them for life or even hang
them. The time had come for him to shoulder the responsibility. He
must educate himself first. 'Study' was the cry that reverberated
through the corridors of his mind. Study to defend the cause of the
downtrodden he had taken up. Study to reply to the arguments
advanced by the critics and study to voice his feelings to buttress
the freedom struggle.

He had learnt a lot from his father who had been banished from
India for his fight against the rulers. His grandfather, a man of
means, openly contributed to the Congress, the only Indian party,
which Bhagat Singh thought had seriously joined issue with the
British.

How could Bhagat Singh forget or forgive the British who had
separated him in his infancy from his father and uncle. When he
was less than 10 years old, Bhagat Singh and his friends had often
formed a contingent which dreamed that it would one day fight
against the British. His mother was often concerned that he might
follow the footsteps of his father or, more so his uncle. She would
tell him: "Bhagatu, you have to look after the family." And at night
she would stealthily go to his bed to ensure that he was not up with
his heavy books or lost in thought. His mother did not like the type
of books he read. She knew for certain that they were not meant for
lessons at school. She was even more worried when he look notes
with reverence.

During the brief imprisonment after the bomb at Dussehra,
Bhagat Singh had protested against the conditions in jail. Two-and-
a-half years later, he found thing worse than before. He could not
bear the animal-like treatment meted out to prisoners. He had then
vainly drawn the attention of the authorities to the tortuous
conditions in prison.

Back in jail, he decided to take up the issue again. He was,
however, convinced that the government would not respond until
he organised a prisoners' agitation. He also wanted to prove to
Gandhi that the revolutionaries also knew how to go through the
rigours of fasting and the torture of approaching death. They too

could suffer the pangs of hunger, something which the followers of non-violence visibly demonstrated.

But before he could plan anything, he was re-arrested for the murder of Saunders. The life imprisonment sentence given in the Assembly bomb case was kept in abeyance until the outcome of the murder trial.

Bhagat Singh had felt something ominous when the Assembly bomb trial was nearing an end. The judge was in a hurry. He even said that Bhagat Singh had been found connected with some other case.

The police had gathered 'substantial evidence' against Bhagat Singh. Police raids at Saharanpur and Lahore had recovered bombs, pistols and cartridges. From Macleod Road at Lahore alone, where Bhagwati Charan lived, 22 bombs were said to have been recovered. Bombs were also found at Jhansi. It was apparent that one of their revolutionary comrades had informed the police about the exact location of the bomb factories. All their work done over the years was exposed.

Still worse was that his colleagues, Jai Gopal and Hans Raj Vohra, had turned government approvers. Those who had fought against the government had become a government instrument to fight the revolutionaries.

Bhagat Singh's involvement was suspected in the killing of Saunders and head constable Charan Singh. Some 21 cases, a few of a serious nature, were registered against him. The authorities had collected nearly 600 witnesses to establish their charges against him.

The authorities knew that Bhagat Singh was not alone. Who were the others? Could they establish a conspiracy and show that the revolutionaries were all together, scheming, planning and executing the killings? How could the government string together their individual acts of violence to establish a well-hatched plot to kill white men?

Whatever the government did, it was conscious of the fact that its image had been tarnished by the one-sided trial in the Assembly case, first before the magistrate and later before the Sessions judge. People, particularly the youth in the country, were convinced that the British had hatched a conspiracy to finish off young radicals. Bhagat Singh was transferred to Mianwali jail and Dutt to Borstal jail in Lahore. Both were put on the same train on March 12 but in different compartments.

Bhagat Singh wondered if the message of the revolution had been understood. It was not the romance the pistol but a self-inflicted ordeal of suffering. Entirely immersed in the society that suppressed him, a revolutionary was capable of changing it. He too was bound by rights and values that were already given but he had to find roads of his own, sometimes through force and sometimes through persuasion. Hunger-strike too was one road.

Demanding an improvement in living conditions in jails was one way of drawing the attention of the authorities. Bhagat Singh decided that he and Dutt should go on a hunger strike on June 15, as soon as they reached their respective jails. But he wondered how to convey the date of the fast to Dutt?

A British officer, who had specially been deputed to keep an eye on Bhagat Singh, said more than once during the journey that a young man like him should not waste his life. Bhagat Singh felt that the officer was tractable. He requested the officer to allow him to travel with Dutt for a short distance since it might be their last journey together. They were old friends and their parting was going to be final. A few farewell moments would in no way violate any rule, Bhagat Singh argued. Nor could they run away because they were handcuffed.

The officer relented and transferred Bhagat Singh to Dutt's compartment up to the next station. Bhagat Singh told Dutt to go on a hunger strike in Borstal jail on June 15 and he would do the same in Mianwali jail.

After reaching Mianwali, Bhagat Singh told his co-prisoners that though the Kakori revolutionaries fought long to improve jail conditions and even extracted a promise on concessions, nothing tangible had materialised. The British had gone back on their word.

The first thing he did when he arrived at the jail was to get hold of a list of the amenities provided to prisoners, both Indian and European. He found that the Europeans got better accommodation, food and daily use items. Maltreatment at the hands of the jail authorities was difficult to quantify, but rations were not.

The prisoners, although detained for political reasons, appeared to have reconciled themselves to the conditions. Bhagat Singh found the members of the Babbar Akali being treated as criminals. Even bare necessities were denied to them. He identified the main problems getting enough rations and a bearable environment as well as ensuring human treatment for the prisoners. Often bread was thrown at them in the way it was flung at animals in cages. The authorities were abusive in their language.

Bhagat Singh took up their cause and proposed a hunger strike in protest—a Gandhian way. He wanted to prove that the revolutionaries were willing to employ any method to fight the British. Days after the hunger strike, he wrote a letter to the jail superintendent on June 17.

"We, as political prisoners, should be given better diet and the standard of our diet should at least be the same as that of European prisoners. (It is not the sameness of dietary that we demand, but the sameness of standard of diet). We shall not be forced to do any hard and undignified labour at all. All books, other than those proscribed, along with writing materials, should be allowed to us without any restriction. At least one standard daily paper should be supplied to every political prisoner. Political prisoners should have a special ward of their own in every jail, provided with the necessities as those of the Europeans. And all the political prisoners in one jail must be kept together in that ward. Toilet necessities should be supplied. Better clothing."

Five

It was strange that till his letter reached the jail authorities, they had taken no notice of the hunger strike. Bhagat Singh had underlined in his letter that "when a European breaks an ordinary law in order to fulfil his selfish motive, he gets all kinds of privileges in jail. He will get a well-ventilated room with electrical fittings, best food, such as milk, butter, toast, meat, etc. and good clothing, while we politicals are deprived of such things"

On the day he wrote to the jail superintendent, he also sent a letter to the Inspector-General (Jails), Punjab:

"Despite the fact that I will be prosecuted along with other young men arrested in the Saunders shooting case, I have been shifted to Mianwali Jail from Delhi. The hearing of the case is to start from June 26, 1929. I am totally unable to understand the logic behind this kind of shifting. Whatever it be, justice demands that every undertrial should be given all those facilities which help him to prepare and contest the case. How can I appoint any lawyer while I am here? It is difficult to keep contact with my father and other relatives. This place is quite isolated, the route is troublesome and it is far from Lahore."

The letter had its effect. Bhagat Singh was shifted to Lahore Central Jail. Little did he realise then that the transfer would be used for ulterior motives.

Before sending him to jail, the authorities took him to the cantonment police station in Lahore. The witnesses, already assembled there by the investigating staff, were allowed to see Bhagat Singh from close quarters so that they would have little difficulty spotting him during the identification parade.

Bhagat Singh continued the hunger strike in Central Jail. Here he met Udham Singh* who told him that he would one day go to London

---

*He shot O'Dwyer dead at Coxton hall in London in March 1940, nine years after Bhagat Singh was hanged. When sentenced to death, Udham Singh said: "I do not care about dying. I am dying for a purpose," more or less the same words which Bhagat Singh used before the hanging.

and kill Michael O'Dwyer, Lieutenant Governor of Punjab when the massacre was committed in Jallianwala Bagh. The hunger strike spread to other jails. Baba Sohan Singh, after serving a sentence of 15 years, was awaiting his release when Bhagat Singh gave the call for the hunger strike. He too went on fast. The authorities punished him by extending his term by another three years.

When the country came to know about the hunger strike, there was wide protest. The Congress took serious note of it. Moti Lal Nehru condemned the government and said: "The hunger strike is for a general cause and not for themselves."

As the fast prolonged without any solution in sight, Jawahar Lal Nehru met Bhagat Singh and the other hunger strikers. He expressed his concern and issued a statement: "I was very much pained to see the distress of the heroes. They have staked their lives in this struggle. They want that political prisoners should be treated as political prisoners. I am quite hopeful that their sacrifice would be crowned with success."

Mohammad Ali Jinnah, who had by then distanced himself from the Congress because of differences over its functioning, raised the matter of the hunger strike in the Central Legislative Assembly. In his speech, he said: "They (Bhagat Singh and Dutt) were not given the treatment — not on racial grounds — but according to the standard and the scale which is laid down for Europeans in the matter of diet and bare necessities of life. It is not a mere question that they want to be treated as Europeans." Jinnah had a dig at the British. "So far as I know, Bhagat Singh and Dutt wore *topees* and their figures appeared in shorts (when they appeared in the public gallery in the Assembly hall). Therefore, they ought to have been treated as European."

Jinnah criticised the government for discriminating between Indian and European prisoners: "You ask me, who is a political prisoner? It is very difficult to lay down any particular definition. But if you use your commonsense, if you use your intelligence, surely you can come to the conclusion with regard to the particular case and say, here are these men who are political prisoners and we do not wish to give them proper treatment. We want to give them treatment as undertrial prisoners. If you had said that, the question would have been solved long ago. Do you wish to prosecute them or persecute them?"

He said: "I regret that, rightly or wrongly, youth today in India is stirred up, and you cannot, when you have three hundred and odd million of people, prevent such crimes being committed, however much you may deplore them and however much you may say that they are misguided. It is the system ... of government which is resented by the people... But, remember, there are thousands of young men outside. This is not only the country where these actions are resorted to. It has happened in other countries, not youths, but grey bearded men have committed serious offences, moved by patriotic impulses..."

There was no response from the government. After many days, it reacted but only to express concern over the health of the hunger strikers, not to concede any demand. The statement made the prisoners more furious and they decided to ignore it. There was no let-up in the hunger strike. Prisoners would often break into groups to talk to one another or join in singing patriotic songs like the one given below:

> Kabhi who din bhi ayega
> Ke jab azad hum honge
> Yeh apni hi zamin hogi
> Yeh apna asman hoga
> Shahidon ki chitaon par
> Lagenge har baras mele
> Watan par marne walon ka
> Yehi nam-o-nishan hoga

(A day will come for us to be free.
It would be our land.
It would be our sky.
There will be fairs held every year at places.
where the pyre of martyrs is lit.
This would be the only remembrance left
of those who died for the country.)

At times, Bhagat Singh engaged the attention of the hunger strikers by urging them to always keep before them the ideals of the movement. The moderates agitated to get sixteen annas but pocketed one anna and fought for the rest. The revolutionaries must always keep in mind that they were striving for a complete revolution, complete mastery of power in their hands. British Labour leaders betrayed their real struggle and had been reduced to mere hypocritical imperialists. Diehard conservatives were better than the polished imperialist Labour leaders.

Revolution, he said, was not a philosophy of despair or creed of desperadoes. It was a vital living force which was indicative of eternal conflict between the old and the new, between life and living death, between light and darkness. There was no concord, no symphony, no rhythm without revolution. Revolution was law, revolution was order and revolution was the truth. Without it, there could be no progress either in nature or in human affairs.

The hunger strike was now on everybody's lips in the country. There was spontaneous sympathy. Many from the public registered their support by going on fast. Some newspapers began publishing a daily health bulletin on the hunger strikers. Many meetings were held to voice protest against the British. At a meeting held at Jallianwala Bagh in Amritsar a warning was administered to the bureaucracy that it would be responsible if any harm came to the prisoners. At another meeting in Lahore, more than 10,000 people raised their hands to express solidarity with the hunger strikers. So wide was the sympathy that June 21 was celebrated as Bhagat Singh Day throughout the country.

Still the government did not relent. More comrades in the jail wanted to take up the challenge and join the hunger strike. Jatindra Nath Das, a young but tough revolutionary, was opposed to the emotional approach. He advised them caution. It would be a long struggle, he warned. "Inching to death in the hunger strike is far more difficult than death in a gunfight or on the gallows," he said. It would be against revolutionary traditions to withdraw a strike without attaining the objective, was the reply of the hunger strikers. "It is better not to join the strike than to suffer a premature withdrawal," Jatindra said. They did not listen to him. He was not against them. But he wanted them to know beforehand how hard the task would be. He led the fast.

The government used several tricks to break the strike. Dishes of different types were placed in their cells and then removed to test the resolve of the hunger strikers. But nobody faltered. Water pitchers in cells were filled with milk so that either the prisoners remained thirsty or broke their fast.

When the government realised that the strike had assumed dangerous proportions, they tried to use the same tricks as they had used to dupe the Kakori railway prisoners — agreeing to concessions but not implementing them. The government announced that it would give better facilities and adequate food to the political prisoners. Some of the hunger strikers were promised special treatment on medical grounds. But nobody was taken in. Bhagat Singh told the authorities that it was all too familiar. The hunger strikers rejected the offer.

The authorities resorted to forced-feeding. The hunger strikers resisted it. The government soon gave up their effort because of the danger involved. One of the prisoners, Kasuri, swallowed red pepper and drank boiling water to clog the passage of the feeding tube. The government saw no course other than compromise. The Governor came down from Shimla to meet jail officials. There was no breakthrough.

The British were forced to appoint the Punjab Jail Enquiry Committee to look into the matter. The Committee gave an undertaking on behalf of the government that a special diet and other facilities would be given to the political prisoners. Some of the hunger strikers broke their fast. However, they sent the committee's chairman, Duni Chand, a note that the strike had only been suspended, not abandoned. The prisoners did not have to wait long to find that the government had gone back on its word.

Bhagat Singh and Dutt were offered the same terms. But they refused to accept them until a gazette notification was issued to make them official. The two had learnt a lesson from the fate of the Kakori prisoners.

When the government discovered that the fast was riveting the attention of the people, it hurried the trial, which came to be known as the Lahore Conspiracy Case. It started in Borstal Jail, Lahore, on July 10, 1929. Rai Sahib Pandit Sri Kishen, a first-class magistrate, was the judge. He had earned the title of Rai Sahib for loyal service rendered to the British.

Bhagat Singh and 27 others were charged with murder, conspiracy and waging war against the king. The average age of the revolutionaries was 22.

The magistrate's court was barricaded by the police. The general public was not admitted. Even the counsel for the accused was stopped from entering. They were allowed to enter only after some delay. Bhagat Singh's parents were among the few visitors.

On their part, the revolutionaries showed no interest in the trial and adopted an attitude of total indifference. They had neither any faith nor any respect for the court constituted by the British. They said the English loved liberty for themselves and hated all acts of injustice, except those which they committed themselves.

Still they wanted to see if they would be proved wrong. They thought they would also show the public that the attitude of the court was pre-determined. A handcuffed Bhagat Singh, still on hunger strike, was brought to the court on a stretcher. His weight had fallen by 14 pounds, from 133 to 119.

By then, Jatindra Nath Das's condition had deteriorated considerably. The jail committee recommended his unconditional release. The government rejected the suggestion on making it a matter of prestige. It offered to release him on bail. But he did not agree. Someone deposited the bail money but Jatin refused to accept it. He was so weak that he could not even turn in bed. The government propagated that he wanted all the hunger strikers, including the ones charge-sheeted, to be released unconditionally. This was not true. He had scrupulously kept the jail facilities separate from the case.

Jatindra was sinking fast. The end could come any day. Bhagat Singh and his comrades felt helpless. The country too waited with a feeling of indignation. Jatin did not give up his fast even though most of his comrades had done so after the jail committee's assurance.

At Bhagat Singh's personal request, he agreed to an enema to clear toxins from his bowels. "Who can say 'no' to Bhagat Singh," he told the jailor. However, Jatin refused to touch any food. Nor did he allow himself to be force-fed. The Bengal revolutionaries had left the cult of the bomb and the pistol. But they had resolved to make themselves an example of sacrifice to tug at people's conscience. Jatin followed the resolve to the very end. The fast lasted 63 days.

Jatin died on September 13. Subhash Chandra Bose, a top Congress leader from Bengal, sent 600 rupees to send his body to Calcutta. Bombay and Punjab too offered money. Jatin's last words were: "I do not want any obsequies to be performed at Kali Bari in the orthodox Bengali fashion. I am an Indian." After his death, the Viceroy informed London: "Jatin Das of the Conspiracy case who was on the hunger strike, died this afternoon at 1 p.m. Last night, five of the hunger strikers gave up their the hunger strike. So, there are only Bhagat Singh and Dutt who are on strike..."

The official announcement on the death was cold and businesslike: "J.N. Das died yesterday at about 1.10 p.m. His brother K.C. Das had received Rs.600 from Subhash Chandra Bose from Calcutta to pay for the carriage of the body by car."

The country fell silent. People felt as if someone from their own family had died. They had followed his long hunger strike with bated breath. Now it was all over. They were sad and sullen but felt proud that he had not failed. It was a vicarious satisfaction for the nation which found in the uncompromising Jatin a winner against the mighty British empire.

The funeral procession started from Borstal Jail at about four in the afternoon, with eighty eminent Punjab Congress leaders and volunteers. But as the procession wended its way to the railway station, hundreds of mourners joined it. Most shops were closed.

The news of Jatin's death spread all over India in no time. There was a sense of loss, but also a feeling of helplessness. People expressed it as they stood silently, bare-headed, at every railway station which the train carrying the body passed.

There were some six lakh people waiting at Howrah station platform and outside. Many more joined in as the funeral cortege moved through the crowds lined on both sides of streets in Calcutta. It took many hours to reach the Hooghly banks where the cremation took place. There were flowers all the way. The walls were pasted with posters saying in Bengali: "Let my son be like Jatin Das." As the pyre was lit by his brother, cries rose into the sky.

The Viceroy informed the Secretary of State in London about the procession through a telegram, saying: "The procession in Calcutta is stated to have been of a record size and to have consisted of five lakhs of people...The crowd was undoubtedly enormous...Meetings of sympathy with Das and of condemnation of the Government have been held in many places, but no report has yet been received of any clash with the authorities."

Highest tributes were paid to Jatin by practically every leader in the land. Two Punjabi leaders, Mohammad Alam and Gopichand Bhargava, resigned from the Punjab Legislative Council in protest. Moti Lal Nehru proposed the adjournment of the house at the Central Assembly as a censure against the government's policy on the treatment of the Lahore prisoners. He accused the government of "inhumanity" and blamed it for adopting an attitude which "resulted in the death of Jatindra Nath Das and endangered the lives of others."

Another member, Neogy, described the Home Member as belonging to "the race of Dyer and O'Dwyer". The censure motion was carried by 55 against 47 votes.

Gandhi did not share the enthusiasm the hunger strike had generated. He disapproved of the publication in the Congress bulletin of Bhagat Singh and Dutt's joint statement which had been thrown as a handbill in the assembly hall. Gandhi expressed his unhappiness in a letter to Nehru, then the Congress General Secretary.

Nehru had to issue a statement in explanation: "As a matter of fact, I am not in favour of the hunger strike. I told this to many young men who came to see me on this subject but I did not think it worthwhile to condemn the fast publicly."

Bhagat Singh felt the loss of Jatin beyond words. He wept, highly emotional as he was, openly. He took out his notebook and recited slowly a passage, which he had captioned: "The noblest fallen."

"The noblest have fallen. They were buried obscurely in a deserted place.

No tears fell over them,

Strange hands carried them to the grave.

No cross, no enclosure, and no tombstone tell their glorious names.

Grass grows over them, a feeble blade bending low keeps the secret.

The sole witnesses were the surging waves which furiously beat against the shore.

But even they, the mighty waves could not carry farewell greetings to the distant home."

The writer U.N. Figner, was relatively less known. But Bhagat Singh felt the words said what he wanted to convey.

Jatin's death only steeled the revolutionaries. They prepared themselves for the next ordeal. They believed that the conspiracy case was a cover by the British to hang Bhagat Singh and some other comrades. They too decided to treat the court proceedings as a farce. It was a charade. Still they wanted to expose the farce in public.

A brain trust of three people was constituted comprising Bhagat Singh, Sukhdev and Bijoy Kumar Sinha to decide on the strategy. They decided that they would not attend the court on some days to let it be known that they did not recognise a foreign power-appointed magistrate to try the freedom fighters. They also decided that on some days they would attend the court only to raise the following

slogans: Long Live Revolution, Down with Imperialism. The slogans
would be followed by a national song in chorus. On some days, they
would attend the court to reiterate their belief that the deliverance
of their country could only come through freedom and revolution.

The proceedings were often disturbed. Since the court faced a road,
students from nearby schools and colleges assemble outside to wait
for Bhagat Singh and his associates. They all joined the
revolutionaries as soon as they began the song:

> *Kabhi wo din bhi ayega*
> *Ke jab azad hum honge*
> *Yeh apni hi zamin hogi*
> *Yeh apna asman hoga*
> *Shahidon ki chitaon par*
> *Lagenge har baras mele*
> *Watan par marne walon ka*
> *Yehi nam-o-nishan hoga.*

On certain days, they would switch to another song.

> *Sarfaroshi ki tamanna ab hamare dil mein hai*
> *Dekhna hai zor kitna bazuai katil mein hai*
> *Waqt ane de bata deinge tujhe e asman*
> *Ham abhi se kya batain, kya hamare dil mein hai.*

(Driven by desire to put my life at stake. I am yet to see how
strong my assassin is. In time you will know the full story. It is too
early to reveal the secret of my heart.)

Often they used the court as a place to expound the ethos of
revolution. First they wanted to liberate India from foreign rule and
then they would transform it into a socialist society. Revolution, as
their party's manifesto said "may be anti-God but is certainly not
anti-man". They were clear that the struggle in India would not end
so long as "a handful of exploiters go on exploiting the labour of the
common people for their own ends". It mattered little whether the
exploiters were British capitalist or purely Indians.

The jail committee requested Bhagat Singh and Dutt to give up
their hunger strike. But it failed to persuade them. Finally, it was
Bhagat Singh's father who had his way. He was armed with a
resolution by the Congress urging them to give up the hunger strike.
The revolutionaries respected the party because they were conscious
of its struggle for India's freedom. They called Gandhi 'an impossible
visionary' but they saluted him for the awakening he had brought
about in the country.

Both Bhagat Singh and Dutt agreed to suspend the hunger strike at the party's request. It was the 116th day, October 5, 1929 and Bhagat Singh had surpassed a 97-day world record for hunger strikes, set by an Irish revolutionary.

While breaking the fast, Bhagat Singh and Dutt sent a message to the Congress: "In obedience to the resolution of the All India Congress Committee, we have today decided to suspend the hunger strike till the final decision by the government in regard to the question of treatment of political prisoners in Indian jails. We are very anxious that all those who went on the hunger strike in sympathy with us should also discontinue it forthwith..."

Bhagat Singh refocussed his attention on the trial. He recalled the first day at the magisterial court when they had raised the slogans, "Long Live Revolution" and "Down With Imperialism", endlessly.

The Crown was represented by C.H.Carden Noad, the Government Advocate, assisted by Kalandar Ali Khan and Gopal Lal, and Bakshi Dina Nath, prosecuting inspector of police. The accused were defended by Duni Chand, Barkat Ali, Mehta Amin Chand, Bishan Nath, Amolak Ram Kapur, W. Chandra Dutt and Mehta Puran Chand.

The court recorded an order prohibiting slogans in the courtroom. But Duni Chand, the defence counsel sitting nearest to the magistrate, pointed out that the wording of the order had been dictated by Kalandar Ali Khan, the public prosecutor. Duni Chand asked if it was part of the duty of the Crown counsel to frame the orders of the court. Did the police rule the court, Duni Chand asked ? Khan, however, denied the charge.

The Government Advocate filed the orders of the government sanctioning the prosecution under the Explosive Substances Act and sections 121, 121A, 122 and 123 of the Penal Code relating to sedition.

Hamilton Harding, the Senior Superintendent of Police, Lahore, filed the formal complaint under the orders of the government. He read out the names of the accused, then the complaint, which alleged the hatching of a conspiracy to wage war against the King.

The accused were also charged with collecting men, arms and ammunitions for overthrowing the government. The complaint referred to the Hindustan Republican Army and their meetings at Lahore and other places in India "with a view to establish a federal republican government in its stead". The revolutionaries gave their reply by raising the slogan, Long Live the Revolution.

Court: "Every sane person would object to such shouts (Slogans)."

Duni Chand objected to the court holding its sittings in a portion of the jail. He said the so-called courtroom was small and it was surrounded on all sides by the police. The relatives and friends of the accused waited outside on the roadside and were not allowed admission.

Court: "Should the whole city come here?"

Counsel: "Everybody who wanted to come should be admitted provided there is room."

Carden-Noad pointed out that no discrimination was made between members of the bar and others or between the prosecuting counsel and the defence counsel. There was not enough room in the hall for all who desired to attend the proceedings.

Counsel Barkat Ali challenged the statement. He pointed out that the Government Advocate and another European came straight in without anyone questioning them or asking them to produce a permit while Ali had been stopped outside the gate. Ali asked the sub-inspector on duty the reason for the discrimination and was informed that the Government Advocate and Europeans did not require a pass.

Carden-Noad at this stage drew the attention of the magistrate to the distribution of flowers among the accused. He said he wanted his objection to be recorded.

The court took notice of Carden-Noad's objection but overruled the protest by the defence counsel regarding the restrictions on admission. The magistrate held that to control congestion and congregation of people it was necessary to regulate admission by passes, but every facility would be given to the relatives of the accused.

The government's decision not to allow many visitors was defeating the purpose of the revolutionaries. They were not getting enough opportunity to disseminate their message. They too took up the matter of entry to the court strongly with the magistrate. The restrictions were relaxed. The youth were allowed in but only in restricted numbers.

At that time, a rumour began that the British and the Congress would reach some sort of compromise. Bhagat Singh cautioned young political workers against the type of assessment which was a let-down. He asked them to work among workers and peasants. The real revolutionary armies were in villages and factories. He advised them to adopt Marxism as their ideology.

Durga Das Khanna, a close friend of the revolutionaries, managed one day to attend the court. Seeing him in the visitors' gallery, Bhagat Singh pushed himself near him and said: "What a fool you are! Why are you here? You leave immediately and should not be seen around here at all."

There was one Sikh Deputy Superintendent of Police, an admirer of the revolutionaries, in the courtroom. He came up to them. He had overheard what Bhagat Singh had told Khanna. The police officer said: "Well, your leader is giving you very sound advice. I am not going to take any action. I would also advise you to leave at once." Indeed, some in the police establishment were sympathetic to the revolutionaries.

The government felt satisfied that the case despite interruptions was on the rails again. Bhagat Singh and his comrades did not think that way. One day they recalled the Kakori prisoners' bravery. On January 21, 1930, the accused appeared in the court wearing red scarves. As soon as the magistrate sat in the chair, they raised the slogans 'Long Live Socialist Revolution', 'Long Live People', 'Lenin's Name Will Never Die' and 'Down With Imperialism'.

Bhagat Singh then read out the telegram which he wanted to be sent to the Third International. The telegram said: "On Lenin Day we send hearty greetings to all those who are doing something for carrying forward the ideas of the Great Lenin. We wish success to the great experiment Russia is carrying out." Little did they realise then that their God would fail 60 years later.

The magistrate went on in a mechanical way with the case. He would listen to complaints and reject them as if he had been instructed to do so. A typical example was that of Prem Dutt Verma, one of the accused. He complained to the court that a police constable, who was on duty to keep guard over him, had used abusive language while addressing him. He requested the removal of the constable. Otherwise, he said, he would be compelled to take the law into his own hands. Mehta Puran Chand, counsel for Dutt; argued that in view of the complaint, the constable should be removed from his present duty.

The court asked how it could be established that the constable had abused the accused. Amolak Ram Kapur, the defence counsel, submitted that the incident had happened only a few minutes before in the open court and there were several witnesses. The matter had been immediately brought to the notice of the court and it was the court's duty to make inquiries. It was a serious matter and if the court refused to look into it, the accused might have to lodge a formal complaint. The court refused to take notice of the matter and proceeded further.

Matters came to a head one day when Jai Gopal, the approver, twirling his moustache, went to the witness box and showered abuses on Bhagat Singh and his comrades. "Shame", "Shame," was the cry from the visitors. Verma, the youngest of the accused, hurled a slipper at Jai Gopal. The proceedings were stopped. The magistrate passed an order that the undertrials should be handcuffed itself in the court. Bhagat Singh declared then and there that they would not attend the court until the order was withdrawn.

After the slipper incident, the prisoners were subjected to untold savagery. The *Young Liberator*, Bombay, wrote: "There is no limit to official brutality and lawlessness. The treatment meted out to the Lahore prisoners may not have been accorded even to medieval brutes and uncivilized barbarians."

The following day the police used force to take the revolutionaries to the court. But it failed to produce even a single undertrial. Out of 16, five were physically lifted and put into the prison van. But they too held on to their seats and did not come out when the van reached the court entrance.

The jail superintendent made a deal with them: the handcuffs would be removed in the court. They agreed to drop their boycott. But they discovered, to their horror, that it was only a ruse. The handcuffs were not removed. They too paid the authorities in the same coin. They requested the removal of their handcuffs during lunch in order to eat. After the meal, when the police tried to handcuff them, they resisted the attempt which led to a scuffle. Some hefty policemen beat them in court before the eyes of visitors.

Bhagat Singh was singled out by the police and pounded upon with sticks and boots. He angrily asked the magistrate: "Have you ordered the police to kick us? Can't you control them?" Verma complained that the policemen had inserted fingers into the prisoners' rectums and that they had kicked them in the testicles. "You call it civilised behaviour?" he asked indignantly.

The magistrate did little. But he had to rescind the order on the handcuffing when the press, including some newspapers in London, reported about the "brutal beating of prisoners."

With the passage of time, the case got publicity beyond the shores of India—something Bhagat Singh and his comrades had wished but did not know that it would happen. Contributions to the HSRA began to pour in from all parts of the country. Indians living in Canada, Japan and America sent donations. One lady from Poland also sent money and wanted to know all about the proceedings.

Photos of Bhagat Singh and Dutt appeared all over the country in homes and shops. Calendars with their pictures did roaring business. There was pride in what the revolutionaries were doing in the court. Many eminent people including Moti Lal Nehru, Rafi Ahmed Kidwai and the raja of a small state in UP, Kalakarkar, visited the court to express their solidarity.

During one of his visits, Moti Lal Nehru praised Bhagat Singh for the admirable work the revolutionaries had done. He said their bravery had brought independence closer. Bhagat Singh utilised his services to make full use of their case to warn the British that the foreign rulers would be the target of the youth till they withdrew from the country. Bhagat Singh knew about two things: a plan to gun down Khan Bahadur Abdul Aziz, the CID superintendent, and the electrically-controlled detonation of a bomb on the Viceroy's train.

As it turned out, both escaped narrowly. The bullet fired at Aziz went astray. A rear carriage of the Viceroy's train was destroyed but the compartment in which he travelled suffered no damage. It was Azad's doing. Bhagat Singh knew of the capabilities of his revolutionary friend.

The attack on the Viceroy came at a time when the hearings in the magistrate's court had lowered the image of the government. The stock of revolutionaries had gone high. One, they were able to expose the fabrication of the case. Two, the impression which got around was that their arms were long enough to reach anyone in the government.

The case built by the prosecution was that a revolutionary conspiracy had been hatched, not when Saunders was murdered but two years earlier in September, 1928. At that time various revolutionary parties had strung themselves together into one organisation to operate in the north and the east of India, from Lahore to Calcutta.

The amalgamation part was correct. Indeed, the HSRA came into being to coalesce the revolutionary activities at different places. But to draw a line between revolutionary activities before 1928 and after was like dividing water. All the revolutionaries, wherever they were, had been working for many years for the same purpose: to change the society.

The case proceeded at a snail's pace. The government got so exasperated that it approached the Lahore High Court for directions to the magistrate: he should have the right to refuse the examination of further witnesses whenever he considered that a prima facie case had been established.

A division bench of the Lahore High Court, headed by Chief Justice Sir Shadi Lal, dismissed the application of Carden Noad. In his judgement, Shadi Lal said: "This is an application under Section 561 of the Criminal Procedure Code, made by the government advocate on behalf of the Crown in a case which is pending before a magistrate. The circumstances under which the application has been made do not admit of any dispute."

The government's prize witnesses were Jai Gopal and Hans Raj Vohra. Both had made confessions and both were members of the Central Committee of the HSRA. Jai Gopal was the first to make a confessional testimony. Bhagat Singh felt personally disappointed because he had described Jai Gopal as 'a jewel' in the party. Jai Gopal recalled how Sukhdev asked him whether he wanted to serve the country. One defence counsel asked him to identify Sukhdev. He pointed his finger towards him. "I will wear *Khaddar* and belong to the Congress," Jai Gopal said.

His purpose was to underline the difference between Gandhi's non-violence and the revolutionaries' faith in violent overthrow of the government and the system. He wanted to disown the past because when he joined the party, he knew what it stood for. Its manifesto opened with the sentence: "The food on which the tender plant of liberty thrives is the blood of the martyr."

Sukhdev, Jai Gopal said, persuaded him to become a member of the secret society, the object of which was to overthrow the government. "I stole for Sukhdev from the school library a book entitled *Manufacture and use of explosives.*"

One incident that Jai Gopal* revealed was that when three or four days after Saunders' murder, he, Sukhdev and Kishori Lal went

---

*This was not true. Sukhdev denied it in a marginal note to the report of the trial proceedings. "Nonsense," he wrote. "As a member of a body, I could not do so." Sukhdev wrote: "I believed him too much. Many a time I disclosed before him what I should not have." All the three—Bhagat Singh, Sukhdev and Rajguru—were given a copy each of the trial proceedings after the hearings were over. Sukhdev was the only one of the three who wrote as many as 241 comments in the margin.

towards the Canal bridge on Ferozepur Road and they found Scott and his wife passing in the car that way. Jai Gopal said that he suggested to Sukhdev that if he desired, 'I can shoot down Scott'. Sukhdev replied that there was no use killing him since luck had saved him once. After Jail Gopal, it was Hans Raj Vohra, who spilled the beans. Vohra too had been pardoned by the magistrate.

For reasons known to the authorities, Duni Chand, Bhagat Singh's legal adviser, was not allowed one day to take his seat in the court —among the defence counsel, nor as a member of the Bar or in the Press gallery. Duni Chand walked out of the court in protest saying: "In no part of the world are the members of the Bar treated in the manner in which they are treated in this court."

The day Duni Chand was insulted, Bhagat Singh and his comrades decided to stay away from the court. They also resumed their hunger strike. They told the magistrate that they had no alternative because the government had gone back on its commitment on better treatment, better facilities and better diet for the prisoners. The *Civil and Military Gazette,* an English daily from Lahore, assailed them for boycotting the court. Bhagat Singh contradicted it and explained the reasons for not attending the court.

In a letter to the magistrate, Bhagat Singh said that after going for the through the *Civil and Military Gazette,* he considered it necessary to explain the reasons for resuming their hunger strike. He complained of the harassment which their supporters had to go through. Their best well-wishers were not allowed to meet them. "I myself," he said, "cannot keep a whole-time lawyer; therefore I wanted that my trusted friends should observe the court proceedings by being present there, but they were denied permission without any explicit reason..."

Bhagat Singh ended his letter with the observation: "We can never like this drama acted in the name of justice, because we do not get any facility or benefit for defending ourselves. One more serious complaint is against the non-availability of newspapers. Undertrial prisoners cannot be treated like convicted prisoners. We should be given at least one newspaper regularly. We want one newspaper also for those who do not know English." He added: "We will rejoin the proceedings when these inconveniences are removed".

Ten days after the hunger strike, on February 19, the government issued a press communique on the classification of convicted and undertrial prisoners. The accused gave up their hunger strike the next day. But the government again went back on its assurances. All the accused were placed in the 'C' class and treated with 'vindictive brutality'.

The series of announcements on facilities and their withdrawal was a part of a long record of the government's perfidy. It wanted to trick the revolutionaries into a situation where they would give up the hunger strike before getting the facilities. The government broke its promise so many times and so unashamedly that even the revolutionaries felt embarrassed.

Throughout March, the proceedings were relatively smooth. But both sides, the authorities and the revolutionaries, had come to realise that they were at the end of the road. The magistrate felt he could not make any headway without the cooperation of the undertrials. They, in turn, were convinced that the proceedings were a sham. It was an ordeal for both of them.

The farce ended on May 1, 1930 when Viceroy Irwin promulgated an ordinance to set up a tribunal to try what was already known as the Lahore Conspiracy Case.

The ordinance put an end to the proceedings pending in the magistrate's court. The case was transferred to a tribunal of three High Court judges without any right to appeal, except to the Privy Council. The tribunal was similar to the one which tried the Ghadarites during the First World War. It was also given powers to deal with wilful obstruction and to dispense with the presence of the accused.

The statement of objectives, issued along with the ordinance, were:
(1) The offences were of an 'unusually serious character.
(2) The conduct of the accused rendered it impossible 'to count upon obtaining a conclusion by the normal methods of procedure within any calculable period.

The Viceroy also blamed the revolutionaries on trial for stalling the proceedings through their hunger strike. Bhagat Singh refuted the charge in a letter to the Viceroy, pointing out the hunger strike had nothing to do with the trial. He said that they would have remained silent if the whole responsibility had not been put on their shoulders.

Bhagat Singh alleged: "It was not the hunger strike that had forced you to promulgate the ordinance. There is something else, the consideration of which confused the heads of your government. It is neither the protection of the case nor any other emergency which forces you to sign this lawless law. It is certainly something different. But let us declare once and for all that our spirits cannot be cowed down by ordinances. You may crush certain individuals but you cannot crush this nation. As far as this ordinance is concerned, we consider it to be our victory."

The appointment of the Tribunal gave a clear message that the British were prepared to do anything to crush any challenge to their rule or the system. It meant trampling upon every canon of justice but the British rulers were clearly prepared for it.

The tribunal was generally seen as an exercise to hang the leading revolutionaries, particularly Bhagat Singh. The youth had come to idolise him. The case put a new life in the freedom movement which had reflected a sense of depression after the failure of the non-cooperation movement. In fact, people were so fired up now that Gandhi found the atmosphere opportune to prepare for the Dandi March for the right to make salt from sea water.

When the appointment of the tribunal was announced in the court, Bhagat Singh thanked the magistrate on behalf of the accused. He told him that they had nothing personal against him. They were free from hate and fear. The prolongation of their harassment, Bhagat Singh assured him, had not made them bitter.

The revolutionaries, who had embarked on the path of 'propaganda by action' — a phrase coined by Sukhdev — felt confident that they were reaching somewhere. Both the Assembly case and the magistrate's court had helped get them attention. They had been able to put across not only the idea of need for the attainment of independence but also for the establishment of a classless society, a concept different from that of Gandhi who wanted the rich to stay but as the trustees of the wealth they produced. The revolutionaries had no doubt that even after the attainment of freedom, the struggle would continue as long as a handful went on exploiting the common people.

The tribunal was only a formality to silence their voice, once and for all. Life or death? What did it matter? They had always scorned the grave. They were out to break the fetters of slavery. They were fighting for the freedom of people all over the world.

Six

May in northern India is oppressive. The monsoon does not break out until two months later. Even the lingering touch of spring in April is well past by that time. Lahore, in fact, swelters in the sun without any respite. On May 5, 1930, all roads should have led to the stately Poonch House, converted into the court. But they did not. People were afraid, even though Bhagat Singh, their hero, and two of his comrades, Sukhdev and Rajguru, were put on trial in public. All the three had taken up the gun to free India from the British yoke.

It was a hot day, the temperature touching 106.3° Fahrenheit. But it was not so much the heat as was the terror that had deterred people from attending the court. Many had preferred to stay back because they had heard that those who went there would subsequently be harassed, along with their relatives.

For many days, the authorities had been picking up people at random. More than 200 of them had been detained on the suspicion that they were sympathetic to the revolutionaries. The city was swarming with turbaned policemen and white officers in Sola-hats.

Poonch House looked like a mini cantonment, heavily guarded with armed policemen. The intelligence department had warned the government against an attempt to rescue Bhagat Singh. Entry was through passes which were issued selectively.

Not even 40 chairs were occupied when the three tribunal members — Justice J. Coldstream, followed by Justice Agha Haider and Justice G. C. Hilton — entered the courtroom two minutes after 10 a.m. In the audience was Kishen Singh, who had constituted a defence committee despite his son's opposition. Bhagat Singh had told his father in vain that political workers must ignore the courts and should be ready to pay the heaviest punishment with a smile on their face.

A large oblong room, with high ceiling of corrugated sheets, served as the courtroom. Placed on a wooden platform was a table. The

Judges sat behind the table in long chairs. Above their heads was a small photo of George V.

A few fans with wooden blades were hanging from the ceiling. Even at full speed, they were not very effective. Visitors mostly used as a fan a photo of Bhagat Singh which had been distributed widely in the city. However uncomfortable they felt, their eyes were fixed not on the dais but on the side-door from where Bhagat Singh and his comrades were expected to enter. They heard the screeching of vans, the shuffling of feet and the raising of slogans. They stood up in respect.

Their heroes, 18 of them, burst into the room, which resounded with *Inquilab Zindabad* and *Gora Jaja , Jaja* (white man go, go).

Bhagat Singh and his associates then broke into a familiar song:

Sarfaroshi ki tamanna ab hamare dil mein hai
Dekhna hai zor kitna bazuai katil mein hai
Waqt ane de bata deinge tujhe eh asman
Ham abhi se kya batain, kya hamare dil mein hai.

The judges sat impassively. The visitors tapped their feet on the floor. Both the revolutionaries and the visitors were in harmony as if the two had become one.

Coldstream, in the chair, summoned Gopal Lal, the public prosecutor, and asked him to provide the tribunal with an authoritative translation of the song. Agha Haider tried to explain the meaning, but his voice was drowned by the song. Coldstream looked towards the police, who awaited his orders.

All of a sudden the song stopped. Rajguru broke away from his comrades and positioned himself opposite the judges behind the specially constructed barricade. He challenged the very constitution of the tribunal. He said it was illegal, *ultra vires*. The Viceroy, he said, had no powers to cut short the normal procedure of the law. The Government of India Act, 1915, authorised him to promulgate an ordinance to set up a tribunal but only when the situation so demanded. No such conditions obtained for his step. There was no breakdown in the law and order situation. Nor had there been any uprising. He had to prove before the court whether an emergencylike situation existed.

Rajguru asked the tribunal to defer the hearings till it was decided whether the Viceroy had the authority to use extraordinary powers in normal times. He was not alone to question the validity of the ordinance. Several other revolutionaries in the dock also backed him.

Five of them also demanded a fortnight's adjournment to enable them to make necessary arrangements for defence.

The tribunal considered the petition as 'premature'. Coldstream also rejected Rajguru's objection, and refused to adjourn the proceedings. He believed all this was part of the 'tactics' that had been used earlier to disturb the hearings before Magistrate Sri Kishen.

Coldstream was determined to reject any objection to proceed further. Equally determined were Bhagat Singh and his comrades not to let the tribunal proceed. It looked as if there was a war of attrition between the two. Once again they raised the slogan Long Live The Revolution to stop the proceedings. Once again Rajguru got up from his seat but this time delivered a speech in Urdu. He lamented that British rule had sucked India's blood and had reduced it to penury and helplessness. He said there was only one form of government, whatever it might be called, where the ultimate control was in the hands of the people.

He was still speaking when Coldstream interrupted him to say that the tribunal did not follow the language in which he addressed it. Rajguru shot back that he too did not understand English, the court language. He wanted an interpreter. Coldstream acceded to his request.

It was a little after 11 a.m. when the case was started. Carden-Noad, the government advocate, asked for leave of the court to state the facts of the case in his capacity as complainant. Malik Barkat Ali, Duni Chand, Mehta Amin Chand and other counsel objected to that they argued that Carden-Noad was not a complainant because he had not taken oath to enjoy that status. Since there was no evidence before the court, it would not be possible to stop the crown counsel if he strayed into irrelevant matter. This was bound to prejudice the defence. The tribunal left the matter at that, without giving any decision on whether Carden-Noad could make a statement without taking oath.

Carden-Noad made the opening speech on behalf of the prosecution and charged Bhagat Singh and his comrades with conspiracy to murder and wage war against the King. He accused them of initiating the cult of the gun which he said had spread throughout the country. Carden-Noad alleged that they had an organisation called the Hindustan Socialist Republican Army, which used arms, bombs and explosives. He charged them with getting money from abroad for their activities. Carden-Noad referred to the

Saunders murder and said it was part of a much wider conspiracy. He mentioned various fictitious names used by the undertrials.

Carden-Noad then elaborated on the charges by mentioning the collection of arms, men, ammunition and obtaining money by robbing banks, treasuries, by dacoities, manufacturing explosive bombs, murdering of police and other officials, blowing up of trains, throwing bombs in the assembly, circulating of seditious literature, rescuing convicts and inducting educated youth were the accomplishments for revolution in India.

Carden-Noad said that there were 28 accused in all. Eighteen were present, five had absconded and five had turned approver. He read out the names of the 18 in the order given below:

1. Sukhdev Alias Dayal, alias Swami, alias villager
2. Kishori Lal Rattan, alias Dee Dutt Rattan, alias Mast Ram Shastri
3. Des Raj
4. Prem Dutt alias Master, alias Amrit Lal
5. Jai Dev, alias Harish Chandar
6. Sheo Verma, alias Parbhat, alias Hamarain, alias Ram Narain Kapur
7. Gya Prashad, alias Dr. B. S. Nigham, alias Ram Lal, alias Ram Nath, alias Desh Bhagat
8. Mahabir Singh, alias Partab
9. Bhagat Singh
10. Ajoy Kumar Ghosh, alias Negro General
11. Jatin Sanyal (Jatindra Nath Sanyal)
12. Bejoy Kumar Sinha, alias Bachu
13. Shivram Rajguru, alias "M"
14. Kundan Lal, alias Partap, alias No.1
15. Kanwalk Nath Trivedi, alias Kanwal Nath Tewari

The evidence of G. T. Hamilton Harding, Senior Superintendent of Police, took the court by surprise. He said that he had filed against the accused, the First Information Report (FIR), "under the instructions of the Chief Secretary to the Government of Punjab. I do not know the facts of the case, nor did I make the statements. I am acting only as a formal complainant under the instructions of the government."

The judges were taken aback. Carden-Noad tried to water down the shack over Hamilton's evidence by talking about the dangers him the accused who were absconding. He said that there was no immediate prospect of arresting Bhagwati Charan, Azad, Kalicharan and Yash Pal.

Hardly had Carden-Noad finished his observations when J. N. Sanyal, one of the accused, rose and said that he proposed to address the court on behalf of the accused, Mahabir Singh, Prem Dutt, Gya Prasad Nigam, Kundan Lal and himself.

Without waiting for the court's permission, he made a virulent attack on the British government. Sanyal said that the British had committed so many murders that it was not possible for Indians to avenge them even if they wanted to do so. Subjugating people was the biggest crime in the world and the British were guilty of it. With their brute force, he said, they had sought to suppress the struggle for man's birthright, freedom.

Raising his voice, Sanyal said that they were not the accused, but the defenders of India's honour and dignity. The accused were those who represented the British Raj. He was reading from a paper which he was trying to finish as quickly as possible. Coldstream stopped him from doing so, observing that reading a paper in an open court was highly improper. He ruled what Sanyal had already read out was entirely irrelevant to the guilt or innocence of the accused and smacked of 'seditious propaganda'. However, he ordered the paper to be placed on record.

When Sanyal was abruptly stopped, there was pandemonium in the court. The hall once again reverberated with slogans, *Inquilab Zindabad*, Down With Imperialism. Sanyal, who was still on his feet, said that "the trial was a sham". "We decline to be a party to this farcical show," he said. "We shall not take part in the proceedings." All the accused joined Sanyal in voicing their protest and informing the court that they would boycott the proceedings.

Before withdrawing from the court all the accused repeated Sanyal's words, "We decline to be a party to this farcical show", and henceforth, "We shall not take any part in the proceedings of the court".

As they were leaving, a small-statured man walked in and said he was the interpreter. He knew Hindi, English and Marathi. It was an anticlimax. The case was adjourned to the following day.

As Bhagat Singh returned to his cell, he recalled how familiar was the tribunal's attitude. The magistrate's court before which they were arraigned earlier behaved in the same manner. There too he had sensed that the judge had already made up his mind.

He had told his colleagues after the magisterial trial that they should take no cognizance of the tribunal. But some among them said that they should participate in the proceedings so that they might make a statement like the one Bhagat Singh made in the Assembly case.

Bhagat Singh was sure that the attitude of the tribunal must have convinced his colleagues about the mockery of the trial. There was no purpose in pursuing the case. He was convinced that their earlier decision to treat the court proceedings as a farce was correct. They should expose the British sense of justice more openly and more persistently.

Bhagat Singh was, however, happy that the audience had been wholeheartedly with them, whether it was the case of Saunders' murder in Lahore or of throwing bombs in the assembly hall in Delhi. He recalled how once when an overzealous approver had made a statement against the revolutionaries, the people in the magistrate's court had shouted 'Shame'

Since the British had already made up their mind to hang them, why should they give credibility to the court by their presence? It was better to boycott the proceedings. Such was the thinking of the revolutionaries. To whatever extent possible, they would expose the travesty of British justice. They should not believe even for a second that they would be able to stall their execution. It was only a question of time. They should be prepared for it. Even otherwise, political workers should not bother about legal fights in courts.

Any defence would make no sense. This was Bhagat Singh's argument before his comrades. He sent a message to his father to wind up the defence committee, which never had his approval in the first place. When he and his colleagues were not sorry for what they had done, then why have a defence committee? Theirs was an ideological stand, deliberate and open.

The issue was not whether a Britisher had been killed but whether the assassination would make London understand that there was a set of determined Indians who would stop at nothing to release not only their own country from bondage but also the shackled people all over the world. The tribunal searched for members of the defence committee who had submitted a petition to intervene but these was no trace of them. Bhagat Singh's father had already complied with his son's wishes and dissolved the committee.

Even after realising that the trial was a sham, Bhagat Singh and. his comrades wanted to see how the tribunal would go about its business to sentence them when there was no evidence, no witness, no proof. Even W.J.C. Fern, a white policeman, who was at the scene of Saunder's murder, had not recognised Bhagat Singh at the identification parade held in jail.

True, there were five approvers.* Three of them — Jai Gopal, Hans Raj Vohra and Phonindro Nath Ghosh—had been associated with them for a long time. But Jai Gopal was only used as a messenger and did not know much about the movement. Vohra was associated more with students and Ghosh had not done any important revolutionary work. How could the corroboration of what one approver said by another approver be sufficient ground for conviction? Their statements could not be regarded as evidence.

The following day, on May 6, when the tribunal reassembled, Bhagat Singh put up an application that he wanted a legal adviser to watch the proceedings and give him advice from time to time. He named Duni Chand, the person who had intervened during the the hunger strike case, as his legal adviser. To make sure that it was only a formality, Bhagat Singh said that the legal adviser would not cross-examine witnesses, or address the court. Carden-Noad did not object to the arrangement. The tribunal readily gave its sanction.

The tribunal formally asked the accused whether they wished to be represented at the expense of the Crown. Nine said "no". Five did not care to reply to the question and four of them agreed to the suggestion. The tribunal recorded their wishes as given below.

1.	Bhagat Singh.	No.
2.	Sukhdev.	No.
3.	Kishori Lal.	Yes, but can name nobody, Wants to consult Kishan Singh, a member of the Defence Committee.
4.	Agya Ram.	No.
5.	Des Raj.	Yes, cannot at present say whom he wants.
6.	Pre Dutt.	Yes, cannot at present say whom he wants. Wants to consult Kishan Singh.
7.	Jai Dev.	No.

*Sukhdev commented on the margin of the case proceedings: "No one but we ourselves through our own failures proved to be the worst enemies of ourselves, hence of the cause. At every step you can find a confession, a statement and even such 'pointing outs'." Sukhdev wrote against the names of many witnesses on the margin: "False witness (FW) Tutored witness (TW)".

8. Sheo Verma.	No.
9. Gya Prasad.	States he will give no reply.
10. B.K. Dutt.	I refuse to answer any question by this court.
11. Kanwal Nath Trivedi.	No.
12. Ajoy Kumar Ghosh.	Yes, cannot say whom until he sees the Defence Committee.
13. Jatindar Nath Sanyal.	States 'I give no reply'.
14. Surinder Nath Panday.	No help from this court.
15. Mahabir Singh.	Says he will take no part in he proceedings.
16. Shiv Ram alias Rajguru.	No help.

For the next few days, the accused came to the court, shouted the slogan, *Inquilab Zindabad*, or hummed the famous tune, *Sarfaroshi ki tamanna ab hamare dil mein hain*, and sat down on the benches. A pattern began to emerge: when the slogans stopped, the judges appeared and when the slogans began, they walked out of the room. Once in a while the judges stayed back, when the slogans were raised, to watch the scene.

One week after the opening of the case, on May 12, Coldstream came to the court before Bhagat Singh and his colleagues entered the dock. As usual, they shouted the slogan *Inquilab Zindabad*. Coldstream ordered them to stop. They refused to obey him. Instead, they raised their voice to the maximum pitch.

At that point, Coldstream asked the police to handcuff them and clear the court. Even the press correspondents were asked to leave. That did not deter them from shouting slogans. Bhagat Singh protested against the handcuffing. Coldstream then recorded an order, which Hilton signed, to handcuff the prisoners and remove them from the court.

The police entered the box where the accused were sitting on benches and began showering lathi blows upon them. They, retaliated with their hands. A serious fight followed. Coldstream sat back and watched as the police dragged them on the floor and forcibly put them in a prisoners' van. In the fight, Bhagat Singh and his comrades were hurt. They announced the boycott of the proceedings in protest. Coldstream's argument was that the slogans and revolutionary songs amounted to contempt of the court. The accused said until Coldstream offered an apology for the beating, they would not recognise the court.

Agha Haider, the only Indian member on the tribunal, was not happy over the beating. He recorded a note: "I was not a party to the order of the removal of the accused from the court to the jail and I was not responsible for it in any way. I dissociate myself from all that took place today in consequence of that (Coldstream's) order."(Sukhdev characterised it as 'praiseworthy' in the marginal note on the proceedings). When the proceedings resumed the next day, Agha Haider made a statement that he dissociated himself from all that had taken place the earlier day in consequence of the order.

The beating looked like a pre-planned job. The Viceroy was getting a daily report. He knew about the boycott of the proceedings. He knew about the slogans. But he did not know that things would come to such a pass where the only Indian judge on the tribunal would record his protest.

The suspicion of the accused that it was only an exercise the British wanted to complete was confirmed. They were shocked when the tribunal did away with the formality of the identification of the accused. Whatever identification had taken place in the court of the magistrate was taken as evidence for the purpose of the tribunal's proceedings as well.

For most of the others, the identification was held in the jail itself. There was a parade of the accused and the witnesses were asked to identify them by name or otherwise. If witness could claim that he had identified the accused in the jail in the presence of the officials, that identification was considered in order.

After the beating incident, all the accused, except Sukhdev from the Borstal Jail, were not produced in the court because they had refused to come unless brought by force. Each of the accused was asked individually to come to the court and they refused. From then onwards, the jail authorities would report on each hearing that the accused had resisted coming before the tribunal. It, in turn, would record the statement of the jail authorities and dispense with the attendance of the accused.

For example, a typical order received by Coldstream on June 18, 1930, said: "Both Bhagat Singh and B.K. Dutt today refused to attend court. Both were brought to the main gate where the Police Inspector took each of them by the arm and ordered them to come to court, whereupon they each refused to move." It was no different on other days.

The tribunal did not suspend the proceedings despite the boycott by Bhagat Singh and his associates. Most Indian lawyers also dissociated themselves from the case. The press too walked out. The tribunal went ahead and recorded the statements of the approvers.

The prosecution case was based mainly on the story that the three approvers — Phonindra Nath Ghosh, Jai Gopal, Hans Raj Vohra — had re-constructed. They were associates of Bhagat Singh and his comrades.The last two were familiar with what went on at Mozang Road house. The government depended on them because it did not have a clue on what the revolutionaries had planned and how they had executed it.

Ghosh concentrated on the amalgamation of provincial revolutionary parties into a single revolutionary party, the Hindustan Socialist Army, Jai Gopal on the murder of Saunders and Vohra on other activities of Bhagat Singh and his comrades. All of them mutilated facts to fit them into the framework of conspiracy which had been hatched to overthrow the government through violence.

Jai Gopal's was a long and tedious testimony spread over 10 days. He told them how in the middle of September 1928 when he was at the revolutionary party headquarters at Ferozepur, Bhagat Singh and Sukhdev came during the night. Bhagat Singh got his *kesh* (long hair) cut off. The beard was also shaved. He dressed himself in clothes as men in UP did in a dhoti and kurta. This was all to escape defection.

Jai Gopal narrated one example of their efforts to collect funds. It was decided to raid the Punjab National Bank in the city. Both Azad and Bhagat Singh would go out practising motor driving on the day when the bank was to be robbed. Bhagat Singh and Pratap Singh were asked to reach the bank at 3 p.m. Kalicharan was to cut the telephone wires. Sukhdev was to snatch the gun from the sentry at the entrance of the bank and Kishori Lal and Jai Gopal were to put currency notes in two bags.

"When I reached the bank I saw Chandra Shekhar, Sukhdev and Hans Raj Vohra," Jai Gopal said. "But by 3 o'clock, Bhagat Singh and Pratap Singh did not arrive with the taxi., They came in a *tonga* and since no arrangements for a taxi could be made, the dacoity was postponed." (After a bank robbery, the revolutionaries would leave a receipt of the amount collected with the remark: "You can encash it after independence")!

"Many days later," Jai Gopal said, "we decided at the Mozang Road house that Scott, Senior Superintendent of Police, should be murdered because he had struck Lala Lajpat Rai with a lathi. I was deputed to identify Scott's car, No. 6728. I watched his movements for three to four days. December 17 was fixed for the murder."

Jai Gopal revealed that Bhagat Singh made a number of posters in thin paper and printed in red. The posters were on behalf of the Hindustan Socialist Republican Army. The original typed version said: "Scott is dead; Lalaji is avenged."

Hans Raj Vohra gave evidence towards the end of May 1930. The government banked on it. During the testimony, the Public Prosecutor asked him: "Previously when you were arrested on December 17, 1928 (the Dusshera bomb blast), in spite of the fact that you were in police custody for seventeen days, you did not divulge any secret of the party. This time you made the statement shortly after you were arrested. What were the reasons?"

Vohra replied: "I should like to submit before this tribunal a statement giving my reasons by which I was guided to give a statement before the police and accept a pardon."

Hilton remarked at this point: "The question is one, the object of which is to test the veracity of the witness, and it should not be allowed to be put in by the examination-in-chief."

Agha Haider said: "It is not open to the prosecution to put this question to the witness. The question is disallowed."

In his testimony, Vohra said he could express himself better in English than in Urdu. He was allowed to do so.

Vohra said Sukhdev was the brother of his wife's uncle. "In our meetings, we began to discuss about the futility of the Congress programme and the necessity under the special circumstances and the justification, both moral and political, of the creation of revolutionary parties. Sukhdev told me that in as much as India had no constitutional means by which to determine her progress, we must necessarily resort to unconstitutional means."

Sukhdev had already been identified by Vohra in the magistrate's court. Vohra said Sukhdev enlisted him a member of the party and had entrusted him with the task of propagating revolutionary ideas by circulating revolutionary litrature amongst the students.

While describing the view of the revolutionaries, Vohra clarified at one stage that when he said 'my clothes', he meant they were being temporarily used by him. "Those clothes were a common property of the party, the members of which did not believe in 'right of property'."

When it came to Saunders' killing, Vohra said that Sukhdev called him on December 1, 1928 in the evening at Lawrence Gardens, Lahore, and from there he took him to the Mozang Road house. "I was present at the house for 20 or 25 minutes. Bhagat Singh told me there that the party wanted to resort to some action and for that purpose, they had summoned some of the members from UP. That is all I was told that day," Vohra said. At this stage Jai Gopal was brought into the court. Vohra identified him.

On December 15, Vohra said: "Bhagat Singh showed me some pink coloured typed posters, the heading of which was in pink print. Their bottom corners were printed on one side with the date and the other with the word, 'commander-in-chief'. The heading of the typed part of the poster was 'Scott is dead. Lalaji is avenged'."

Vohra admitted that Bhagat Singh had told him that the party had decided to murder Scott for showering lathi blows on Lajpat Rai "which was a sort of challenge to the revolutionary party". Vohra said he agreed to the proposal to shoot Scott dead. He, however, said that he was never informed where the murder would take place. He passed the place, where the crowd was, purely by chance.

The tribunal, even after Vohra had turned approver, tried to show how independent it was.The questions it asked Vohra were:

Q. "Did the keeping away from you of the details of the Saunders murder come to your knowledge after the murder or before the murder?"

A. "Before the murder."

Q. "Did you protest that you were not being let into the secrets?"

A. "I was not expected to protest, nor was I expected to ask any such searching questions from them according to the discipline of the party."

Q. "What was the occasion for Sukhdev to let you into the secret of the places to which the various alleged murderers were sent by the party?"

A. "There was no particular occasion that I can allude to."

Q. "Was it a case of pure and simple outburst of confidence?"

A. "Yes."

After the testimony of the approvers, Khan Bahadur Abdul Aziz was the first witness. He was Superintendent of Police, Montgomery, when he was put in charge of the investigation of the Dussehra bombing. He had also investigated the Lahore Conspiracy Case. He said it was during his searches that he became aware of Bhagat Singh and Babu Singh, members of the Naujawan Bharat Sabha. Babu Singh, Aziz said, offered to give information if he was given 1,000 rupees. Babu Singh revealed that Bhagat Singh was one of the killers of Saunders and also gave information about the formation of a secret society. Aziz said he ordered the arrest of Bhagat Singh there itself but Bhagat Singh had disappeared by then, only to surface on April 8, 1929 at Delhi. Aziz also revealed how he discovered the secret bomb factory in Lahore at a house in Kashmiri Buildings and raided it on April 12, 1929. He said Sukhdev, Kishori Lal and Jai Gopal were arrested from the Kashmiri Buildings where a lot of incriminating evidence was unearthed.

On May 30, approver Ram Saran Das retracted his statement and said that it had been made at the instance of the police. He had made a statement before the magistrate on June 11, 1929. It was later changed by the police and he was made to sign the altered statement.

Because of the boycott of the accused, the proceedings were unreal. The British wanted a way out. Bhagat Singh and his comrades said they would attend the court if Coldstream was removed. He was sent on a long leave and the dissenting member, Agha Haider, was also dropped from the reconstituted tribunal. Two new members, J.K. Tapp and Abdul Qadir, were appointed. Hilton took over as the chairman on June 21. The accused said that Hilton should not be made the tribunal president since he had concurred with Coldstream on the beating of the revolutionaries.

In a joint letter to the Commissioner of the Special Tribunal, Bhagat Singh and Dutt protested that the judge who was party to the order of beating had been appointed as the president. "In these circumstances we want to emphasise one thing that we had absolutely no grudge against the person of. Justice Coldstream. We had protested against the order passed by the president on behalf of the majority and the subsequent maltreatment meted out to us…"

The objection to Hilton was rejected. The proceedings started without the presence of the accused and their lawyers. However, when the new tribunal met, one day after its constitution on June 21, almost all the accused voluntarily came to court. This was after the lapse of six weeks. Agya Ram alone refused to attend. He did not recognise the tribunal or the court.

Again, on June 23, all the accused, except Agya Ram, appeared before the tribunal. He had resisted his forcible production. The tribunal passed an order dispensing with his attendance. However, the proceedings of two days convinced the revolutionaries that there was no difference between the tribunal headed by Coldstream and the one headed by Hilton. They resumed their boycott.

The following day, 13 of them did not attend. The tribunal again passed orders condoning their absence. On June 25, none of the accused was present. The tribunal followed a similar procedure and proceeded with the case in their absence. On July 10, the charges were framed against 15, discharging three.

As the prosecution produced more witnesses and indulged more in fantasy than facts, it became evident that the government wanted to put the noose around Bhagat Singh's neck. On his part, he did not offer any defence. His father became so nervous that he submitted on September 20 a petition to the tribunal, with a copy to the Viceroy, to establish that Bhagat Singh was not in Lahore on the day of Saunders' killing. The burden of the petition was that Bhagat Singh was in Calcutta on the day of Saunders' murder. Bhagat Singh disowned it.

When the tribunal found that the accused had boycotted the proceedings, it ordered that they be brought by force. This had been tried earlier. No amount of violence could bring them to the court. The beatings had no effect. The tribunal ultimately conceded that their presence was not necessary and proceeded with the case.

Now Bhagat Singh, spent most of his time in the cell. There was not even a formality of appearance in the court. He read a lot. He copied one day the following passage from an old book by Charles Fourier (1772-1837) in his notebook:

> "The present social order is a ridiculous mechanism, in which portions of the whole are in conflict and acting against the whole. We see each class in society desire, from interest, the misfortune of the other classes, placing in every way, individual interest in opposition to public good. The lawyer wishes litigation and suits, particularly among the rich; the physician desires sickness. (The latter would be ruined if everybody died without disease as would the former if all quarrels were settled by arbitration.) The soldier wants a war, which will carry off half of his comrades and secure him

promotion; the undertaker wants burials; monopolist and forestallers want famine, to double or treble the prices of grain; the architect, the carpenter, the mason, want conflagration that will burn down a hundred houses to give activity to their branches of business."

The tribunal's proceedings were now a bigger farce than before. It was like Hamlet without the Prince of Denmark. What legitimacy would the case have when even the presence of Bhagat Singh, Sukhdev and Rajguru was not considered necessary? The proceedings seemed a formality.

The tribunal realised that the conspiracy story was weak in the absence of corroborators. True, Jai Gopal and Hans Raj Vohra, from different backgrounds, said more or less the same thing. But both were approvers was not sufficient to justify the conviction of any accused present without any corroboration from an outside source. Since the tribunal could not get any such evidence, it said that there was no ostensible ground for disbelieving the facts stated by the two approvers.

The tribunal mostly used Section 9(1) of the Ordinance dispensing with the attendance of the accused. On July 10, 1930, by an order of the tribunal, copies of the charges framed were served on the 15 accused in the jail, together with copies of an order intimating them that their pleas would be taken on the charges the following day. That day, on July 11, the accused again resisted their production in the court, which directed that all the 15 accused should be deemed not to plead guilty in respect of heads of charges framed against them.

However, on the same day, an order was passed assigning the case to the following day with the direction that all the accused would be required at the commencement of the next hearing. They would then state whether they intended to cross-examine any of the witnesses whose evidence had already been recorded. No accused came to the court. All of them resisted forcible attendance the tribunal passed an order recording that none of the accused had appeared or expressed any wish for cross-examining any witness.

There was practically no proceeding between July 12 and August 4. On August 4, the evidence of medical officers was recorded and they said that all the accused, except Prem Dutt and Kundan Lal, were on the hunger strike and that they were too weak to appear before the tribunal. Once again their presence was dispensed with. On August 11, the tribunal recorded that Bhagat Singh, Sukhdev and Bijoy Kumar Sinha were fit to attend the proceedings but they had refused to do so.

On August 26 — by then 457 witnesses had been examined — the public prosecutor said he would not produce more witnesses and closed the case from his side. The tribunal then adjourned the case to August 27, asking that the accused might he wanting to put questions on the case.

The tribunal passed a separate order under Section 256 of the Criminal Procedure Code calling upon all accused persons to attend the proceedings on the following day. A copy of the order was served to each one of the accused in the jail. On August 28, all the accused resisted presence before the tribunal as before. No defence witness appeared, no list was put up for any defence witness to be summoned on their behalf. The tribunal was adjourned. On August 29 and 30, it was similarly adjourned, without transacting any business.

On September 1, all the accused again resisted production before the tribunal. Their attendance was dispensed with till September 5. On September 5, Amolak Ram Kapur appeared for two of the accused, Bijoy Kumar Sinha and Ajoy Kumar Ghosh, and made an ordinary application before the tribunal for the recall of all the 45 prosecution witnesses for cross-examination. The five approvers — Jai Gopal, P.N. Ghosh, Man Mohan Bannerjee, H.R. Vohra and Lalit Mukherjee — in the custody of the court should also be summoned for cross-examination, Kapur demanded.

Jai Gopal was actually put in the witness box, but Kapur, the defence lawyer, declined to cross-examine him and stated that he had no instructions to cross-examine the approvers. Later, Kapur reappeared before the tribunal and brought an application signed by Bijoy Kumar Sinha and Ajoy Kumar Ghosh asking for a week's adjournment before beginning the cross-examination of any of the prosecution witnesses. The request for adjournment was refused as 'dilatory'. Kapur then withdraw from the court.

The trial was long and protracted, beginning on May 5, 1930, and ending on September 10, 1930. It was a one-sided affair. Even then the case took nearly four months to complete. The accused did not attend most of the hearings. Nor did they defend themselves.

The prosecution presented the statements of the seven approvers and confessions by three unknown accused. There were 450 odd witnesses who claimed to have identified the various accused at different times. There were experts of handwriting, of printing, of arms and ammunition and of explosives.

The tribunal framed charges against 15 of the accused. Agya Ram and Surendra Pandey were discharged. The case against Batukeshwar Dutt was withdrawn as he had already been sentenced to transportation for life in the Assembly Bomb case.

In a letter to Dutt, Bhagat Singh worte: "...You will live and, while living, you will have to show to the world that the revolutionaries not only die for their ideals but can face every calamity. Death should not be a means to escape the worldly difficulties. Those revolutionaries who have by chance escaped the gallows, should live and show to the world that they can not only embrace the gallows for the ideal but also bear the worst type of tortures in the dark dingy prison cells."

Finally, on October 7, 1930, about three weeks before the expiry of its term, the tribunal delivered its judgement, convicting all the accused except three. The three — Ajoy Ghosh, Jatindra Nath Sanyal and Des Raj — were acquitted.

Bhagat Singh, Sukhdev and Rajguru were sentenced to death by hanging. Kishori Lal, Mahabir Singh, Bijoy Kumar Sinha, Shiv Verma, Gaya Prashad, Jai Dev and Kamalnath Tewari were sentenced to transportation for life. Kundan Lal was sentenced to seven years' rigorous imprisonment and Prem Dutt to five.

The 300-page judgment went into the details of the evidence and said that "Bhagat Singh's participation in the Saunders murder is the most serious and important fact proved against him and it is fully established by ample evidence..."

The evidence that Bhagat Singh took part in the Saunders murder was assumed to be supported by three points: one, the evidence of various eyewitnesses, who claimed to have identified Bhagat Singh; two, the statements by the two approvers, Jai Gopal and Hans Raj Vohra, 'who were with him as participants in the murder', and, three, the posters (Scott is Dead) 'were written and proved to be so by the handwriting experts.'

Since the accused had boycotted the proceedings, they came to know about the sentences from a special messenger who brought

the tribunal's order to the jail. The warrants for the execution of
Bhagat Singh, Sukhdev and Rajguru were marked with a black
border.

For some reason, Sukhdev expected life transportation. That meant
staying in jail for another 14 years. Sukhdev wrote to Bhagat Singh
that he would commit suicide if convicted for life. Sukhdev wanted
either release or death, no middle course.

Bhagat Singh said in reply that things people hated outside had
now become essential for them. "For example," he said, "I believed
in personal life, but now this feeling has ceased to occupy any
particular position in my heart and mind. While outside, you were
strongly opposed to it but not a drastic change and radicalisation in
your ideas".

Bhagat Singh reminded Sukhdev that he once abhorred the idea
of suicide but he had now made an about-turn. "May I ask you
whether the situation outside the jail was any lot more favourable
to our ideas? Even then, could we have left it because of our failures?
Do you mean to imply that had we not entered the field, no
revolutionary work would have taken place at all?" He advised
Sukhdev: "Serve, serve and live to struggle for the cause."

The news of the death sentence came as a shock to people. There
were spontaneous hartals and processions in protest all over the
country. Meetings were held in big cities to condemn the ex-parte
sentence. Despite the imposition of Section 144 of the Criminal
Procedure Code, there were hundreds of gatherings where virulent
speeches were made against the British. At several places, the police
lathi-charged even the women. A DAV College professor and 80
students were assauled by a sergeant when they were protesting.

At Lahore, the students took the lead. All colleges were closed,
except the government college where the sons of the elite studied.
There was picketing at the government college. At Bradlaugh Hall,
where Bhagat Singh had addressed many meetings, students and
young men and women passed a resolution praising him and the
others for their "brave sacrifice". The Mori Gate meeting beat all
previous crowd records. It was presided over by the daughter of the
late Lala Lajpat Rai.

The undertrials of the Chittagong Armoury Raid Case sent an
appeal to Gandhi to intervene. So did Surendra Mohan Ghosh, who
presided over a mammoth meeting at Calcutta. At the Buxa Camp,

where leading revolutionaries of Bengal were detained, a resolution was passed requesting the Viceroy to commute the death sentence. A public petition signed by thousands of people was sent to him making the same request.

A defence committee was constituted in Punjab to file an appeal to the Privy Council against the sentence. Bhagat Singh and his comrades were not in favour of that. But they were persuaded on the plea that it would expose the British before the world and show what inhumanities the political prisoners in India had to face. Bhagat Singh's only satisfaction was that the appeal would draw the attention of people in England to the existence of the HSRA.

The proceedings before the five-judge Bench of the Privy Council in London were surprisingly short. In the case, Bhagat Singh Vs. The King Emperor, the point raised by the appellants was that the ordinance promulgated to constitute a special tribunal for the trial, was invalid. It deprived the accused of his right of appeal to the High Court which they would otherwise have had. The government argued that Section 72 of the Government of India Act, 1915, gave the Governor General unlimited powers to set up a tribunal.

D. N. Pritt, who appeared on behalf of Bhagat Singh, said that the legislative power of the Governor General was subject to three conditions: one, there must be an emergency; two, the ordinance must be for the peace and good government of the British India; and three, the ordinance must be within the legislative power of the Indian legislature. "None of these conditions existed," said Pritt.

The prosecution, Pritt said, was to prove that an emergency existed, but it had failed to do so. There was no emergency within the meaning of Section 72. The statement by the Governor General, which accompanied the ordinance, did not show any emergency.

Pritt said what the government had done was to deprive the accused the right to have a *prima facie* case made against them and had denied them the access to a sessions judge and a jury of assessors the right and to High Court at Lahore on appeal. They had been tried before a special tribunal without knowing what the case was against them except as and when it came out of the mouths of approvers or independent witnesses, as the case might be.

The Privy Council dismissed the case Judge Viscount Dunedin, who read the judgment, said that the only case made was that Section 72 of the Act did not authorise the Governor General to constitute a special tribunal. The judge said that a state of emergency did not permit any exact definition. It connoted a state of matters calling for drastic action which had to be judged as such by someone.

"It is more than obvious that someone must be the Governor General and he alone. Any other view would render utterly inept the whole provision. Emergency demands immediate action and that action is prescribed to be taken by the Governor General."

As regards the argument that the ordinance was not conducive to peace and good government of British India, the judge said that "the Governor General is also the judge of that. The power given by Section 72 is an absolute power without any limits prescribed, except only that it cannot do what the Indian Legislature would be unable to do..."

Judge Viscount Dunedin, who had Lord Thankerton, Lord Russel of Killowen, Sir George Lowndes and Sir Dinshah Mulla on the Bench, added that the Governor General was not in any way bound under the law to expound the reasons which induced him to promulgate the ordinance.

Seven

The appeal to the Privy Council aroused some hope. A few thought that the highest court of justice in England might undo the wrong of the tribunal's severe sentences against Bhagat Singh, Sukhdev and Rajguru. Once the death penalty was confirmed, the hanging was only a matter of time. All around there was anger and despondency.

Once again, there were demonstrations all over the country. The streets reverbrated with slogans of *Bhagat Singh, Sukhdev, Rajguru Zindabad*. A song specially composed for the occasion was on everybody's lips:

Bhagat Singh ke khoon ka asar dekh lena
Mitadenge zaalim ka ghar dekh lena.

(You will see the effect of Bhagat Singh's execution we shall destroy the home of the tyrant).

A procession of two lakh people marched through the streets of Lahore to stage demonstration. Bhagat Singh's comrades outside the jail did not give up. They proposed a scheme to rescue the three — a group of revolutionaries would bomb their way through the stone wall and shoot their way out. Vishwanath Baishampayan, Sukh Desraj, the relatively less known revolutionaries, and Bhagwati Charan were to be the members of the advance guard. The scheme never took off. A bomb with a loose pin exploded in the hands of Bhagwati Charan in a practice session which he held across the Ravi. He died before the other two could arrange medical care.

But the would-be rescuers had not realised a that Bhagat Singh did not want to be released in that manner. He did not want to let down the Deputy Superintendent of Jail, Khan Bhadur, who had come very close to him during the 400 days he had spent in the jail. Khan Bhadur had even arranged for Bhagat Singh and his two comrades a farewell dinner with the jail functionaries.

The disappointment deepened as days went by. All eyes were on Gandhi. His pact with the Viceroy Irwin was on the anvil. Although, people realised that Gandhi was opposed to the method of the bomb or the bullet, they believed the situation was different now. It had passed the stage of wrong or right, moral or immoral. It was a stern reality which did not brook discussion or delay. Bhagat Singh and his comrades had to saved.

None denied that the revolutionaries represented a different philosophy. They signified a different route. Non-violence was the anti-thesis of violence. If Gandhi was the sun on the political sky of India, Bhagat Singh was a spark which arose from the depths of dusk. Why should Gandhi hesitate to support those who were in no way less fired than him in the struggle for freedom? At stake were the three lives, not any philosophical treatise.

Gandhi looked like agreeing to a settlement with the government under which the Congress would cooperate with the British in its scheme towards limited participation in the governance. The Viceroy was indebted to Gandhi because London was considering his transfer for not having created conditions for a peaceful rule. One word from Gandhi to the Viceroy was enough to get their sentences commuted, people thought.

Bhagat Singh was, however, keen on the hanging because of the fillip it would give to their ideas. The young men would try to emulate them—those who died to make India free and just. But he wanted the sentence to be postponed for some time so that the reasons for their sacrifice would sink into people's minds deeply. The country, which was at present in the midst of agitations and lathi-charges, might not realise the impact of their hanging as it otherwise would have.

Bhagat Singh was also confident that Gandhi's pact with the Viceroy would be a let-down. When signed, it would arouse more anger. Bhagat Singh wished that the hangings should take place at a time when the Congress would lay exposed and the revolutionaries strengthened. The three corpses would then lie between the people and Gandhi's settlement with the viceroy.

Bhagat Singh was confident that the concept of social justice had won many supporters in the country. Stretching from the last quarter of the nineteenth century to the early part of the twentieth, there were two broad phases: the pre-Gandhian and the Gandhian. The revolutionary movement, though present in both these phases, was not central to either, although they provided the engine-power.

The phase of the revolutionaries started when the moderates were on the decline. But the revolutionaries were like flares which got extinguished after lighting the sky for a while. The reprisal by the government made their duration short. Their efforts to harm the British armoury became stronger. The revolutionaries had made a remarkable comeback when the complacency and conservatism of the Congress caused widespread frustration among the people. The people had great expectations. When they were not fulfilled, they revolted.

The failure of the 1857 revolt dealt a major blow to the Indian hopes to oust foreign rule. It also marked the last time that the Indians were to go to the battlefield in a medieval mindset — soldiers on horseback, flashing swords, rampaging elephants, individual acts of bravery but little concerted action. The revolt made the Indians realise that, for the time being at least, the British might could not be challenged effectively on the battlefield.

Developments of a completely different kind began to transform important aspects of Indian life. There were things like revivalism of the Hindus, the spread of English education, the rise of the middle class, slow industrialisation, the emergence of the Indian press and the integration of the area called India.

Some of these developments took the form of protest against the British. This gave birth to national consciousness. The sense of togetherness began emerging as also the desire to oust the British. In the beginning, protests took the shape of political associations led by the middle class. Their demands were prayers and petititons, articulated by speeches and articles. Some of them began a militant religious revivalism, which was hostile to the western presence. Many of these religious leaders propagated a return to the ideals of the pure Hindu culture, inspired by the Gita and Vedic texts.

It was not one event which marked the beginning of another. There were many small incidents. Coming as they did at a time when the economic condition was rapidly worsening, they only served to inflame passions. Many Indian leaders of the period pointed out the pitfalls of rapid commercialisation of agriculture, destruction of cottage industries, de-industrialisation and then industrialisation only up to a certain point which only served to further the improverishment of India. In spite of the country's abject poverty, the British regularly presented surplus budgets. This gross callousness of the British about the living conditions of the people, especially during times of famines — (there were 10 major famines between 1860 and 1910) — made the people extremely angry and ready to take up arms.

Newspapers too played an important role. They strongly advocated independence, demanded rights for the Indians, urged the nation to wake up and participate in the struggle. Among the prominent newspapers were *Sandhya* (edited by Brahmomadhab Upadhayaya), *Bande Matram* (Bipin Chandra Pal), *Karma Yogin* (Aurobindo Ghosh), *Sanjibani* (Krishna Kumar Mitra), *Bangadarshan* (Bankim Chandra Chatterjee), *Amrita Bazaar Patrika* (Sisir Kumar Ghosh and Motilal Ghosh) and *Jugantar* (Barindra Kumar Ghosh).

Bhagat Singh realised that the radicals were quite successful in pointing out the drawbacks of the moderates. In place of Gandhism, socialism had come to appeal to many. Yet they had failed to find or provide anything which could create conditions like the ones which made the French or Russian revolution possible. They had a long way to go. They must stress the need to do more than just propagate, agitate and make speeches — they wanted self-sacrifice from the youth, a militant programme of resistance, the boycott of foreign goods, and the like. Would their hanging broadcast the ideals they cherished?

Lost in such thoughts and in ferocious reading of books Bhagat Singh little realised how quickly the time had gone by. One day he was visited by Asaf Ali and his wife, Aruna, in his cell. He was then singing, using handcuffs as an instrument to beat time. They asked him if he wanted anything. He smiled in reply and showed them what he had just written in his notebook from *India Old or New*.

> "How many of the Western-educated Indians who have thrown themselves into political agitation against the tyranny of the British bureaucracy have ever raised a finger to free their own countrymen from the tyranny of those social evils? How many of them are entirely free from it themselves, or, if free, have the courage to act up to their opinion?"

Asif Ali told him that the Congress had almost negotiated a settlement with the British. This would create an atmosphere of conciliation. The hangings would not fit into that scenario.

After the two went away, Bhagat Singh addressed a letter 'to young political workers'. He warned them: "The term revolution is too sacred, at least to us, to be so lightly used or misused. But if you say you are for the national revolution and the aim of your struggle is an Indian republic of the type of the United States of America, then I ask you to please let me know on what forces you rely that will help you bring about that revolution. The only forces on which you can rely to bring about any revolution, whether national or the socialist, are the peasantry and the labour. Congress leaders do not dare to organise those forces."

Bhagat Singh said: "If anybody has misunderstood me, let him amend his ideas. I do not mean that bombs and pistols are useless, rather the contrary. But I mean to say that mere bomb-throwing is not only useless but sometimes harmful. The military department of the party should always keep ready all the war-material it can command for any emergency. It should back the political work of the party. It cannot and should not work independently."

Bhagat Singh and Sukhdev were shocked when their relatives asked them to file a mercy petition. How could they even suggest it? Apparently, they were oblivious of their dreams and what they were trying to achieve. They were not even appreciative of the trail they wanted to leave behind for the youth.

The idea of a mercy petition made them write a joint letter to the Governor of Punjab through the jail superintendent.

The letter, dated March 20, 1931, three days before the execution, said: "With due respect we beg to bring to your kind notice the following — "That we were sentenced to death on 7th October, 1930 by a British court, L.C.C. Tribunal, constituted under the Special L.C.C. Ordinance, promulgated by H.E. The Viceroy, the head of the British Government in India, and the main charge against us was that of having waged war against H.M. King George, the King of England."

"The above mentioned findings of the court presupposed two things: First, that there exists a state of war between the British nation and the Indian nation and, secondly, that we had actually participated in that war and were, therefore, war prisoners. The second presupposition seems to be a little bit flattering, but nevertheless it is too tempting to resist the design acquiescing in it…"

"Let us declare that the state of war does exist and shall exist so long as the Indian toiling masses and their natural resources are being exploited by a handful of parasites. They may be purely British capitalists or mixed British and Indian, or even purely Indian. They may be carrying on their insidious exploitation through mixed or even purely Indian bureaucratic apparatus. All these things made no difference…

"As to the question of our fate, please allow us to say that when you have decided to put us to death, you will certainly do it. You have got the power in your hands and the power is the greatest justification in the world. We know the maxim 'Might is right' serves as your guiding motto. The whole of our trial was just a proof of that. What we wanted to point out was that according to the verdict of your court we had waged war and we are therefore war prisoners. And we claim to be treated as such, i.e., we claim to be shot dead instead of being hanged. It rests with you to prove that you really meant what your court had said. We request and hope that you will very kindly order the military department to send its detachment to perform our execution."

The three had come to the conclusion that the Congress leaders, although sympathetic to them during the trial, did not think of "the homeless and penniless workers" when negotiating for more powers from the British. The three did realise that the revolution which they preached had not made progress either. But they were confident it would take different shapes at different times. It could be open, hidden, agitational or fierce. The war would go on till the present social order was completely replaced by a new social order, devoid of exploitation.

They had heard of the noble sacrifice of Bhagwati Charan. They had also heard that Azad had not surrendered to the police when surrounded. He had fought them single-handed and died a hero's death. Their time, too, was almost up, they thought. Was it the end of the HSRA when the British had smashed all their underground factories and arrested their comrades, some of whom had joined the enemy? There was relentless repression. Was it all over — the revolutionaries' struggle of militant nationalists? Bhagat Singh had no doubt that some others would rise and evolve their own methods to free people from slavery and exploitation.

He rummaged through his notebook and read an excerpt, captioned *The Prisoner*: "It is suffocating under the low, dirty roof; my strength grows weaker year by year. They oppress me, this stony floor, this iron chained table, this bedstead, this chair, chained to the walls, like boards of the grave. In this eternal dump, deep silence one can only consider oneself a corpse."

People in the country still had expectations that some sort of agreement would be reached in the ongoing talks between Irwin and Gandhi. When the text of the pact was published, without any reference to Bhagat Singh or the others, the outcry was loud and shrill.

The public was visibly disturbed when the Congress working committee endorsed the Gandhi-Irwin pact on March 4, one day before it was signed. Progressive forces termed the pact as a 'betrayal'.

Ever since the sentence was announced, efforts to at least commute the death sentence had been going out. A petition under *habeas corpus* act that the accused had been 'illegally detained' by the government was rejected by the Lahore High Court. So was another petition to approach the Privy Council to reconsider its earlier decision.

Gandhi began to be blamed. When he came to attend a public meeting in Delhi on March 7, a leaflet was distributed to the audience which read: "Where is peace today? Search the hearts of the mothers whose sons have fallen victims to the bullets, or are still awaiting gallows. Ask the wives of those husbands who have left them widows or are serving life-long imprisonment in the dungeons of a foreign bureaucracy. Do you remember your duty to the martyrs? Will you be partners to such an ignoble pact?" Gandhi did not react to what was said.

Appeals from all over India, from all sections of people were pouring in, usually addressed to the Viceroy, asking him to stay the execution. Madan Mohan Malviya sent a telegram to the Viceroy which read: "May I appeal to your Excellency to exercise your prerogative of mercy in cases of Bhagat Singh, Rajguru and Sukhdev to commute sentences of death passed upon them into those of transportation for life... Execution of these young men whose action was prompted not by any personal or selfish consideration but by a patriotic impulse, however misguided, will give a great shock to the public feeling in the country...Such an act of mercy on your Excellency's part will, at this juncture, produce a very beneficial effect on Indian public opinion."

Two petitions were sent by Vidyavati, Bhagat Singh's mother on February 17 and 19 which said: "Pray stay execution death sentence passed on my son Bhagat Singh by Special Tribunal appointed under Ordinance three of 1930. I petition for mercy on grounds of youth of Bhagat Singh and special circumstances of the case. Detailed petition being submitted through post."

A public memorial was also sent to the Viceroy which read: "May it please your Excellency, we the undersigned request that the death sentences passed by the tribunal at Lahore on Messrs Bhagat Singh, Sukhdev and Rajguru be commuted." Hundreds of people had put their signature.

On March 20, Subhash Chandra Bose speaking at a meeting at Azad Maidan in Delhi said: "The whole of India knows by this time that Bhagat Singh and his comrades, Rajguru and Sukhdev, are going to be executed before long. I must say that the news came as a terrible shock to me when I alighted at Delhi Station yesterday noon... We demand with one voice and one will that the death sentences on Bhagat Singh and his comrades be at once commuted. Bhagat Singh is today not a person but a symbol. He symbolizes the spirit of the revolt which is abroad in the country. We may condemn his methods, but we cannot ignore his selflessness..."

The same day on March 20 a delegation from the Naujawan Bharat Sabha met Gandhi and sought his help in the commutation of the sentence.

The relatives of the three were asked to be present on the morning of the 23rd for the last meeting, as the press said. Almost all relatives — this time also those of Sukhdev and Rajguru — came but only a few were granted permission. They protested, saying all of them would meet or none at all. The relatives were not given any definite information about the time or the place of execution. For the people outside the Lahore Jail, the day ended without any concrete information coming from any government official or anybody else. The relatives just waited.

It was apparent that Gandhi did not want to identity himself with the revolutionaries because that would negate his whole stand. But he did not want them to be hanged. His worry was that many people believed that he had taken no initiative to get the death sentence commuted to life imprisonment. The Viceroy after his talks with Gandhi, wrote: "In conclusion, not connected with above (talks on the pact), he (Gandhi) mentioned the case of Bhagat Singh. He did not plead for commutation. But he did ask for postponement in the present circumstances."

In greater detail, the Viceroy* wrote on March 19, four days before the execution: "As he (Gandhi) was leaving, he asked me if he might

---

*Irwin, who was later honoured by the British, became Lord Halifax. In his memoirs he wrote thus: "If the young man was hanged, said Gandhi, there was a likelihood that he would become a national martyr and the general atmosphere would be seriously prejudiced... Gandhi said that he greatly feared, unless I could so something about it, the effect would be to destroy our pact. I said I should regret that no less than he, but it would be clear to him there were only three possible courses. The first was to do nothing and let the execution proceed, the second was to change the order and grant Bhagat Singh a reprieve, the third was to hold up any decision till after the Congress meeting was well over. I told him that I thought he would agree that it was impossible for me from my point of view to grant him his reprieve..."

mention the case of Bhagat Singh, whose execution on March had been reported in the press." According to the Viceroy, Gandhi said: "This was an unfortunate day as it coincided with the arrival of the new President (of the Congress) in Karachi and there would be much popular excitement." The Viceroy's note said: "I told him that I had considered the case with most anxious care, but could find no grounds on which I could justify to my conscience commuting the sentence... He appeared to appreciate the force of the argument and said no more."

One day later, on March 20, Gandhi met Herbert Emerson, the Viceroy's adviser, who recorded Gandhi's feelings thus: "Gandhi did not seem to be particularly concerned in the matter. I told him that we should be lucky if we got through without disorder and I asked all that he could to prevent meetings being held in Delhi during the next new days and to restrain violent speeches. He promised to do all he could."

Indeed, Gandhi was concerned. His letter to the Viceroy on March 23 showed his concern.

"Dear Friend,

"It seems cruel to inflict this letter on you, but the interest of peace demands a final appeal. Though you were frank enough to tell me that there was little hope of your commuting the sentence of death on Bhagat Singh and two others, you said you would consider my submission of Saturday. Dr. (Tej Bahadur) Sapru (a liberal leader) met me yesterday and said that you were troubled over the matter and taxing your brain as to the proper course to adopt. If there is any room left for reconsideration, I invite your attention to the following."

"Popular opinion rightly or wrongly demands commutation. When there is no principle at stake, it is often a duty to respect it."

"In the present case, the chances are that, if commutation is granted, internal peace is most likely to be promoted. In the event of execution, peace is undoubtedly in danger."

"Seeing that I am unable to inform you that the revolutionary party has assured me that, in the event of these lives being spared, that party will stay its hands, suspension of sentence pending cessation of revolutionary murders becomes in my opinion a pre-emptory duty."

"Political murders have been condoned before now. It is worthwhile saving these lives, if thereby many other innocent lives are likely to be saved, and maybe even revolutionary crime almost stamped out."

"Since you seem to value my influence such as it is in favour of peace, do not please unnecessarily make my position, difficult as it is, almost too difficult for future work."

"Execution is an irretrievable act. If you think there is the slightest chance of error of judgment, I would urge you to suspend for further review an act that is beyond recall."

"If my presence is necessary, I can come. Though I may not speak, I may hear and write what I want to say (Being Monday, it was his silence day)."

"Charity never faileth,"

I am,

Your sincere friend

On that very day the Viceroy wrote lack:

"I have again thought very carefully over everything that you have said and the last thing I should wish to do would be to make your task, especially at this juncture, more difficult. But I am afraid, for the reason I sought to explain fully to you in conversation I cannot see any way to feel that I would be right to take the action you request..."

Eight

March 23 began like any other day when the political prisoners were let out of their cells in the morning. They normally remained out during the day and returned after sunset. But today, when warden Charat Singh showed up around 4 p.m. and asked them to get back in, they were surprised.

It was too early for them to be locked up. They had often tarried behind, long after sunset despite the warden's rebukes. But this time he was not only strict he was also adamant. He would not say why. All that he muttered incoherently was: "Orders from above."

The prisoners had become fond of Charat Singh. He left them alone and never checked what they read. Although some books against the British had been smuggled into the jail he did not confiscate them. He knew that the prisoners were not children. They had delved deep into politics. The books would not make them foment trouble in the jail.

His parental care touched them. They respected him and addressed him as Charat Singh Ji. If he was asking them to get back to their cells, he must have a valid reason, they told themselves. One by one, all of them, went back inside four hours before normal.

Still they wondered why, as they peered out from behind the bars of their cells. Then they saw barber Barkat visiting one cell after another. Bhagat Singh and his comrades would be hanged tonight, he whispered. Could he fetch them Bhagat Singh's comb, pen, watch, or anything they could treasure as a memento they asked.

Always smiling, Barkat was visibly sad. He went into Bhagat Singh's cell and returned with a comb and a pen. Everybody staked their claim. Two out of 17 were lucky after a draw to hand out Bhagat Singh's possessions.

They fell silent; nobody even tried to strike up a conversation. All of them looked towards the passage outside their cells as if they expected Bhagat Singh to walk that way. They recalled how one

day when he came their way, one political prisoner asked him why
the revolutionaries did not defend themselves. Bhagat Singh said
that they must die because they represented a cause which would
get strengthened only by their sacrifice, not through defence in the
court. This evening they were keen to catch a glimpse of the
revolutionaries. But they waited in the hush of the evening,
straining their ears to pick up any sound.

Pran Nath Mehta, Bhagat Singh's lawyer, was allowed to meet
him two hours before the hanging. His plea was that he wanted to
know his client's final wish and it was accepted. Bhagat Singh was
moving up and down in the cell like a lion in a big cage. He
welcomed Mehta with a broad smile and asked him whether he
had brought his book, *The Revolutionary Lenin*. Bhagat Singh had
sent Mehta a message to get him the book because its review in a
newspaper had impressed him.

When Mehta gave him the book, he was very happy and began
reading it as if he was conscious that he did not have not much time
left. Mehta asked him whether he would like to give any message
to the nation. Without taking his eyes away from the book, Bhagat
Singh said: "Convey the two slogans—*'Down With Imperialism'* and
'Long Live Revolution'."

Mehta: "How are you today?"

Bhagat Singh: "Happy, as always."

Mehta: "Do you desire anything?"

Bhagat Singh: "Yes, I want to be born again in this country so
that I could serve it."

Bhagat Singh asked him to thank Pandit Nehru and Babu
Subhash Chandra because both of them had shown great interest
in his case. Mehta also met Rajguru who said: "We shall meet
soon." Sukhdev reminded Mehta to take back from the jailor a
carrom board Mehta had given him a few months earlier.

Soon after Mehta's departure, the authorities told all the three
that the time of hanging had been advanced by 11 hours. Instead
of 6 the next morning, it would be at 7 p.m. today. Bhagat Singh
had hardly finished a few pages of the book.

"Wouldn't you allow me to finish one chapter?" he asked.
Instead, they asked him to move towards the gallows.

All the three locked their arms and strode behind the sentries
leading them to the scaffold. They broke into the familiar
revolutionary song:

Kabhi who din bhi ayega
Ke jab azad hum honge
Yeh apni hi zamin hogi
Yeh apna asman hoga
Shahidon ki chitaon par
Lagenge har baras mele
Watan par marne walon ka
Yahi' nam-o-nishan hoga.

They were weighed, one by one. All of them had gained weight. They bathed and put on black robes but did not cover their faces.

Charat Singh whispered into Bhagat Singh's ears to pray to *Wahe Guru*. He laughed and said: "All my life I have never prayed. As a matter of fact, I have many a time abused God for the miseries of the poor. If I were to ask now for His forgiveness, He will say, 'Here is a coward who seeks forgiveness because his end has come'."

Bhagat Singh made a loud speech which the prisoners could hear in their cells. "The real revolutionary armies are in the villages and in factories, the peasantry and the labourers. But our bourgeois leaders do not and cannot dare to tackle them. The sleeping lion once awakened from its slumber, shall become irresistible even after the achievement of what our leaders aim at."

"Now, allow me to state the case in the simplest manner. You cry 'Long Live Revolution'. Let me assume that you really mean it. According to our definition of the term, as stated in our statement in the Assembly Bomb Case, revolution means the complete overthrow of the existing social order and its replacement with the socialist order... For this purpose we are fighting to handle the government machinery. All along we have to educate the masses and to create a favourable atmosphere for our social programme. In the struggles we can best train and educate them.

"Crush your individuality first. Shake off the dream of personal comfort. Then start to work. Inch by inch you shall have to proceed. It needs courage, perseverance and very strong determination. No difficulties and no hardships shall discourage you. No failure and betrayals shall dishearten you. Through the ordeal of sufferings and sacrifice you shall come out victorious. And these individual victories shall be the valuable assets of the revolution..."

The scaffold was old, but the hefty hangmen were not. All the three men sentenced to death stood on separate wooden planks, with a deep ditch running below them. Bhagat Singh was in the middle. The noose was tightened around each one's necks. They kissed the rope. Their hands and feet were tied. The hangmen pulled the rope and removed the rafters from under their feet. It was a crude mechanism.

The bodies, limp and drooping, remained hanging from the scaffold for a long time. They were brought down and examined by a doctor. He pronounced all three dead. One jail officer was so moved by their courage that he deferred the order to identify the dead. He was suspended then and there. A junior officer did the job instead. Two British officers, one of them the Superintendent of the Jail, supervised the hanging and certified the deaths.

The prisoners in the cell, in the twilight of evening, waited for the sound of steps on the passage opposite their cells. Nobody had come that way for more than two hours, not even the warden to re-check the lock.

The jail gong struck six when they heard at some distance a hushed voice, the thud of heavy boots and familiar snatches of a song: *Sarfaroshi ki tamanna ab hamare dil me hein*. They also broke into another song: *Mai rang de mera basanti chola* (Mother, prepare my clothes for martyrdom). And then there were slogans: *Inquilab Zindabad* and *Hindustan Azad Ho*. The prisoners, too, shouted slogans. So loud was their response that they missed part of Bhagat Singh's speech.

All was quiet now. Long after the hanging, Charat Singh came and burst into tears. In his 30 years of service, he said, he had seen many executions but never had anyone mount the gallows so courageously and smilingly as the three did. The nation's three flowers had been plucked and crushed. But little did the prisoners realise that the saga of their bravery had written the epitaph of British rule.

On August 15, 1947, some 16 years later, the last English soldier left Indian shores. As Bhagat Singh had predicted, the cause would triumph one day. But they had to die to keep the torch of freedom burning.

**** **** ***

The three young men were now only three bodies on the floor, awaiting disposal. Hundreds of people waited outside the thick walls of the jail, keeping a constant vigil. The problem the authorities now faced was to get rid of the bodies. The idea of a cremation inside the jail was given up when the authorities realised that the crowd outside would attack if it saw smoke or the glow of fire.

The authorities demolished part of the jail's rear wall. When it became really dark, a truck was brought and the bodies were thrown into it like pieces of luggage. First, the venue of the cremation was the banks of the Ravi. But the water in the river was shallow. Then it was decided to go to the Sutlej. White soldiers escorted the truck as they drove to Ferozepur, near the Sutlej. But the scheme misfired.

The bodies were not cremated properly. People in the countryside and village Gandha Singh Wallah could see the pyres burning. Many came running to the spot. Soldiers rushed to their vehicles, leaving the bodies as they were, and sped back to Lahore. The villagers reverently collected the remains.

The news of the execution spread like wildfire in Lahore and other cities of Punjab. Young men took out processions throughout the night shouting 'Inquilab Zindabad' and 'Bhagat Zindabad'. There was a *hartal* in the city. Fruit shops and *the subzi mandi* (vegetable market) downed their shutters. Schools and colleges, except the toady government college, remained closed. Police pickets were set up to guard government buildings and Civil Lines where officers lived.

Around noon, notices signed by the District Magistrate, were pasted in various parts of Lahore, announcing that the bodies of Bhagat Singh, Sukhdev and Rajguru had been cremated according to Hindu and Sikh rites on the banks of the Sutlej. This was, however, challenged by several meetings where it was said that the bodies had not been properly cremated. The magistrate issued a denial but nobody took it seriously.

By that time the remains of the three executed men had reached Lahore. A mourning procession had started from *Neelagombad*, not far from the place where Saunders was shot dead. Thousands of Hindus, Muslims and Sikhs participated in the over three-mile procession. Many men wore black bands and women black *saris*.

The processionists shouted slogans such as *Inquilab Zindabad, Bhagat Singh Zindabad.* The entire place was awash with black flags. Passing through The Mall, the procession stopped in the middle of Anarkali Bazaar. The crowd was hushed into silence by the announcement that Bhagat Singh's sisters had reached the city from Ferozepur with the remains of the three men. ˙

Three hours later, the three flower-decked coffins, followed by Bhagat Singh's parents, joined the procession. Loud cries rent the sky. People wept openly.

The procession, ironically, reached the banks of the Ravi, where the authorities had wished to cremate the bodies 24 hours earlier. A mammoth meeting was held in Lahore, condemning the execution and characterising it as illegal. Indignation was expressed over the manner in which the authorities disposed of the bodies. Maulana Zafar Ali Khan, a renowned editor of an Urdu daily, recited a poem to describe how the charred remains of the dead bodies were left under the open sky.

As the news of the execution spread, the nation went into mourning. To express then grief, people took out processions and shut their businesses. The British stayed indoors. Jawaharlal Nehru was the first to pay his tributes. He said that Bhagat Singh was a clean fighter who faced the enemy in the open field. He was a young boy full of burning zeal for the country. He was like a spark which became a flame in a short time and spread from one city of the country to the other dispelling the prevailing darkness everywhere.

Gandhi was profuse in his praise for the courage of the executed. He said: "Bhagat Singh and his companions have been executed and have become martyrs. Their death seems to have been a personal loss to many. I join in the tributes paid to the memory of these young men. Bhagat Singh and his two associates have been hanged. Many attempts were made to save their lives, and even some hopes were entertained, but all was in vain. Bhagat Singh did not wish to live. He refused to apologise and declined to file an appeal. If at all he would agree to live, he would do so for the sake of others; if at all he would agree to it, it would be in order that his death might not provide anyone to indiscriminate murder...".

But these words were lost on many people, who were angry with Gandhi for not having done enough to save the three.

Nine

A pall of gloom hung over the Moti Lal Nehru *pandal* at the annual Congress party session at Karachi. When the session was scheduled for March 29, 1931 nobody had an inkling that Bhagat Singh, Sukhdev and Rajguru would be hanged six days ahead of schedule. A procession of president-elect Sardar Vallabhbhai Patel was abandoned in grief. Reception Committee Chairman Choithram P. Gidwani said in a welcome speech that the tragic news had "plunged the whole country in sorrow and indignation".

Before the execution of the three men, there was widespread hope among people that their lives would be spared. This was natural in the wake of the Gandhi-Irwin Pact and the reconciliation between the Government of India and the Congress.

Bose was also a witness to the euphoria, as he went across to Bombay to meet Gandhi and travelled back with the Mahatma to use the opportunity to discuss the impact of the pact on the eve of the 1931 Congress session at Karachi. Belonging to the 'left wing' of the Congress, he was not in favour of the pact; but people felt otherwise. He found that Gandhi's popularity had reached the high watermark and surpassed even the record of 1921.

At the session, Bose could see disappointment in the eyes of the youth, who wore black bands. They really felt let down. They wanted to know what the Congress had done to save the lives of the three men. Their feeling was that Gandhi had not tried enough. Had he threatened to abrogate his pact with Irwin, the British would have commuted the death sentence to life imprisonment.

Bose had told Gandhi that they should, if necessary, break with the Viceroy on the question of Bhagat Singh and his two comrades. "Because the execution was against the spirit, if not letter, of the Delhi pact." Still Bose said: "It must be admitted that he (Gandhi) did try his very best."

Gandhi's secretary Mahadev Desai also quoted the Mahatma as saying in Gujarati: "I was not here to defend myself and hence I have not placed the facts as to what I have done to save Bhagat Singh and his comrades. I have tried to persuade the Viceroy with all the methods of persuasion that I had. After my last meeting with the relatives of Bhagat Singh, on the appointed date, that is, 23rd morning, I wrote a personal letter to the Viceroy, in which I had poured in my whole being—heart and soul —but it has all gone in vain... The attempt that human mind with all its feelings and sentiments can do was not done by me alone. Pujya Pandit Malaviyaji and Dr Sapru also did their utmost."

Faced with an ugly mood, Congress leaders tried to come up with several explanations. But nothing worked to soothe frayed tempers. One explanation they offered was that Irwin promised Gandhi he would commute the death sentence to life imprisonment but he went back on his word when senior British ICS officers threatened to resign *en bloc* if the three men were not hanged.

An incredible story was that the Viceroy had sent commutation orders to Lahore Central Jail through a telegram. But the bureaucrats joined hands to delay its transmission and jail officials received the telegram after the hanging.

In an appeal to mollify the anger of most Congressmen, Patel paid glowing tributes to Bhagat Singh and his comrades in his address and expressed the deep resentment in the country over the execution. But he spoke Gandhi's language when he said: "I cannot identify myself with their methods. I have no doubt that political murder is no less reprehensible than any other; but the patriotism, the daring and the sacrifice of Bhagat Singh and his comrades command my admiration."

Slogans like *Bhagat Singh Amar Rahe, Inquilab Zindabad* resounded through the air outside the *pandal* as Patel spoke. He said: "The heartless and foreign nature of the government was never more strikingly demonstrated than in their carrying out the executions in the teeth of the all but universal demand for the commutation of the death sentence. Let us not, however, be deterred from our purpose in a fit of resentment. This insolent exhibition of their armed power but adds to the heavy indictment against the soulless system and increases our capacity for vindicating our position if we would refuse to be deflected from the straight and narrow path we have chosen."

Gandhi's statement, after the execution, was distributed again. "Bhagat Singh and his comrades have been executed and have become martyrs. Their death seems to have been a personal loss to many. I join in the tributes paid to the memory of these young men. And yet I must warn the youth of the country against following their example. We should not utilise our energy, our spirit of sacrifice, our labours and our indomitable courage in the way they have utilised theirs. This country must not be liberated through bloodshed."

"About the government I cannot help feeling that it had missed a golden opportunity, to win over the rebels to its side. At least from the point of view of the settlement, it was its duty to postpone indefinitely the carrying out of the death sentence. The government has by its own act dealt a severe blow to the settlement and has shown its capacity to disregard public opinion once again and to exhibit the enormous strength it possesses."

"The reliance on violence is perhaps ominous and suggests that in spite of high sounding and pious proclamations, it does not want to part with power. But the people's duty is clear."

"The Congress must not swerve from the path it chalked out for itself. According to my view, notwithstanding the gravest provocation the Congress should endorse the settlement and test its capacity to secure the results hoped for..."

"...Hence though we praise the courage of these brave young men we should never countenance their activities. By hanging these men the government has demonstrated its own brute nature, it has provided fresh proof of its arrogance resulting from its power by ignoring public opinion. From this hanging it may be concluded that it is not the intention of the Government to part with any real power to the people. The Government certainly had the right to hang those young men. However, there are some rights that do credit to those who possess them if they are enjoyed in name only. If a person exercises all his rights on all occasions, in the end they are destroyed. On this occasion, the Government would have brought credit to itself if it had not exercised its rights and this would have been highly useful in maintaining peace."

"However, it is obvious that the Government has not to date developed such discretion. It was given a clear reason for the public to get enraged. If the latter shows anger, it will lose the games which it is bound to win. Some officials may even hope that the public will give vent to its anger. Whether they do so or not, ours is a straightforward path. While negotiating the settlement, Bhagat Singh's hanging was weighing upon us. We had hoped that the Government would be cautious enough to pardon Bhagat Singh and his associates to the extent of remitting the sentence of hanging. We should not break the pledge we have taken just because our hopes have not been fulfilled, but should bear this blow which has fallen upon us and honour our pledge. By doing so under even such trying circumstances, our strength to get what we desire will increase rather than decrease, while, if we break our pledge or violate the truce, we shall suffer loss of vigour, loss of strength and it will add to our present difficulties in reaching our objective. Hence our *dharma* is to swallow our anger, abide by the settlement and carry out our duty."

In an interview to the press in Karachi, three days before the Congress session, Gandhi said:

"I failed in my efforts to bring about the commutation of the death sentences on Bhagat Singh and his friends and that is why the young men vented their wrath against me. I was quite prepared for it. Although they were incensed against me, they gave vent to their wrath in what I would call a most dignified manner. It was open to them to do physical injury but they refrained from doing so. It was open to them to insult me in many other ways, but they confined their resentment and insult to handing me black cloth flowers representing, I imagine, the ashes of the three patriots. These also they could have showered on me or thrown at me instead of which they gave the option of receiving the flowers from their hands which I did gratefully. Of·course they shouted 'Down with Gandhism', 'Go back Gandhi'."

"This I consider to be a legitimate expression of their anger. Having been used to such an exhibition and that in a much worse and serious form, I was unruffled and took these insults as only a mild expression of their deep grief and anger. I am only hoping that they will exercise the restraint that they did yesterday throughout the INC (Indian National Congress) session for they know I am trying to reach the same goal with them. Only I am following a method wholly different from theirs. I have not a shadow of doubt that as time goes they will discover the error of their ways. Whatever may be true of other countries, in this country which is teeming with famished millions, the cult of violence can have no meaning. In this country of self suppression and timidity almost bordering on cowardice we cannot have too much bravery, too much self-sacrifice. One's head bends before Bhagat Singh's bravery and sacrifice. But I want the greater bravery, if I might say so without offending my young friends, of the meek, the gentle and the non-violent, the bravery that will mount the gallows without injuring, or harbouring any thought of injury to a single soul."

Later, journalists asked Gandhi two questions:

The first question was: did the execution of Bhagat Singh and his friends alter his perspective on the settlement?

"My own personal position remains absolutely the same, though the provocation has been of the most intense character. I must confess that the staying of these executions was no part of the truce, and so far as I am concerned, no provocation offered outside the term will deflect me from the path I had mapped out when I agreed to the settlement."

The second question was: did he think it impolitic to forgive a government which was guilty of a thousand murders?

"I do not know a single instance where forgiveness has been found so wanting as to be impolitic."

But no country has ever shown such forgiveness as India is showing to Britain.

"That does not affect my reply. What is true of individuals is true of nations. One cannot forgive too much. The weak can never forgive. Forgiveness is the attribute of the strong."

Sensing that there was a pronounced anti-Gandhi feeling at the session, Nehru hailed Gandhi as "the greatest apostle of non-violence in the 'World'." But Nehru also warned: "Our way is not Bhagat Singh's way. We have always declared that we cannot free our country by the use of arms." He openly said that "only by the method of Gandhi will the country gain freedom. If we leave the path of non-violence, we shall not be free for years to come".

Nehru sponsored a resolution which was seconded by Madan Mohan Malaviya.

The resolution said: "This Congress while dissociating itself from and disapproving of political violence in any shape or form, places on record its admiration of the bravery and sacrifice of the late Sardar Bhagat Singh and his comrades, Sukhdev and Rajguru, and mourns with the bereaved families the loss of these lives. This Congress is of the opinion that this triple execution is an act of wanton vengeance and is a deliberate flouting of the unanimous demand of the nation for commutation. This Congress is further of the opinion that the government has lost the golden opportunity of promoting goodwill essential at this juncture and of winning over to the method of peace the party, which being driven to despair, resorts to political violence."

Nehru was particularly chosen to pilot the resolution because he was popular among the youth. Patel was heckled. What acted as a catharsis was a speech by Bhagat Singh's father, Kishen Singh. Delegates wept loudly and openly as Kishen Singh recalled Bhagat Singh's words:

"Ham se Bhagat ne kaha tha, ke tum pareshan na ho.
Mujhe phansi lagne do, yehi thik hai. Hamein phansi
lagi to ek hafte main hi swaraj mil jayega. Woh kehta tha ke
Privy Council mein jane se koi faida nahin chunke ghulamon ka
haq nahin hai ke shikayat karein."

(Bhagat Singh told me not to worry. Let me be hanged. One week after the execution, the country will get independence. He warned me against going to the Privy Council because he said slaves had no right to complain.)

Kishen Singh complained about how he and other members of his family were not permitted by the jail authorities to meet Bhagat Singh a day before the execution. "He was there, we could see him. But the police did not allow us to meet him. We just waved hands. How could they do this to a father whose son was being snatched away before his eyes."

But he made a fervent appeal: "You must support your general (Gandhi). You must support all Congress leaders. Only then will you be able to win independence for the country."

Despite its positive tone on Bhagat Singh and his comrades the resolution, was not appreciated by many members. One delegate moved an amendment for the deletion of the following words from the resolution: "Whilst disassociating itself from and disapproving of political violence in any form or shape." He said that the honour to Bhagat Singh, Sukhdev and Rajguru should be given without any qualification. "Having actually lived the life of a non-violent follower of Gandhiji, I claim that it is now derogatory to the sense of dignity and nobility of the house to say that we all stand against any form or shape of violence," said Shastri.

Another delegate seconded the amendment. He said: "The prominent leaders have praised bravery of Bhagat Singh and his comrades. But I do not understand why their action has been assessed in a contemptuous way. Whatever they have done, they have done for the sake of the country."

Before any other delegate rose to speak on the amendment, there was a move for closure. Many hands went up in Shastri's support. It was obvious that Gandhi had not liked the amendment. The resolution Nehru moved had been drafted with Gandhi's approval. Gandhi wanted the amendment to be withdrawn. But some pressed for a vote. The amendment was lost.

The support of the Congress was too crucial for Gandhi to be watered down because of the hangings. He had already agreed in principle to the Round Table Conference at London for a 'settlement'. He had to have the full and unfettered support of the Congress. Jamnadas Bajaj, the Congress party's treasurer let the cat out of the bag when he told Gandhi: "You cannot go to the Round Table Conference hedged round with conditions and tell the world that you are still sticking to independence."

In the *Young India* of June 11, 1931, Gandhi said: "I had interested myself in the movement for the commutation of the death sentence on Bhagat Singh and his comrades. I had put my whole being into the task." In another public utterance, he said: "I would gladly have surrendered my life to the Viceroy to save Bhagat Singh and others."

Surprisingly, Gandhi refused to associate himself with the move to raise a memorial to Bhagat Singh.

The session was still going on when Mathura Das, Sukhdev's brother, delivered a letter by Sukhdev to Gandhi's private secretary, Mahadev Das. The letter had been written just a couple of days before the hanging. Sukhdev had heard that Gandhi was negotiating with the government for the release of prisoners not convicted of violence. At the same time, Gandhi was also appealing to the revolutionaries to stop their movement.

Sukhdev addressed Gandhi as 'Most Gracious Mahatmaji'.

"Since your compromise you have called off your movement and consequently all of your prisoners have been released. But what about the revolutionary prisoners? Dozens of *Ghadar* party prisoners imprisoned since 1915 are still rotting in jails; inspite of having undergone the full terms of their imprisonment scores of martial law prisoners are still buried in these living tombs and so are dozens of Babbar Akali prisoners. Deogarh, Kakori, Machhua Bazar and Lahore Conspiracy Case prisoners are amongst those numerous still locked behind bars. More than half a dozen conspiracy trials are going on at Lahore, Delhi, Chittagong, Bombay, Calcutta and elsewhere. Dozens of revolutionaries are absconding and amongst them are many females. More than half a dozen prisoners are actually waiting for their executions. What about all of these people? The three Lahore conspiracy case condemned prisoners, who have luckily come into prominence and who have acquired enormous public sympathy, do not form the bulk of the revolutionary party. Their fate is not the only consideration before the party. As a matter of fact their executions are expected to do greater good than the commutation of their sentences."

"But, in spite of all this, you are making public appeals, asking them to call off their movement. Why should they do so? You have not mentioned any very definite things. In these circumstances your appeal means you are joining hands with bureaucracy to crush the movement. And your appeals amount to preaching treachery, desertion and betrayal amongst them. If that were not the case, the best thing for you would have been to approach some of the prominent revolutionaries and talk over the whole thing with them. You ought to have tried to convince them to call off their movement. I do not think you also share the general conservative notion that the revolutionaries are devoid of reason, rejoicing in destruction and devastation. Let us inform you that in reality the case is quite contrary. They always consider the pros and cons of every step they take and they fully realise the responsibility which they thus incur and they attach greater importance to the constructive phase of the revolutionary programme than to any other, though in the present circumstances, they cannot but occupy themselves with the destructive part of their programme."

"The present policy of the government towards them is to deprive them of the sympathy and support of the masses which they have won in their movement, and then crush them. In isolation they can be easily hunted down. In face of that fact any sentimental appeal to cause demoralisation amongst their ranks would be utterly unwise and counter-revolutionary. It would be rendering direct assistance to the government to crush them."

"Therefore we request you either to talk to some revolutionary leaders—they are so many in jails—and come to terms with them or to stop these appeals. Please, for goodness sake, pursue one of these two alternative courses and pursue it wholeheartedly. If you cannot help them, then please have mercy on them. Let them alone; they can better take care of themselves, they know that the hegemony of the revolutionary party in the future political struggle is assured. Masses are rallying around them and the day is not far off when they will be leading the masses under their banner towards their noble and lofty ideal—the socialist republic".

"Of, if you seriously mean to help them, then have a talk with them to understand their point of view, and discuss the problem in details."

"Hope you will kindly consider the above request and let your view be known publicly."

Sukhdev ended the letter thus: 'Yours, One of the many'.

Since Sukhdev asked Gandhi to react to his letter publicly, the Mahatma did so. He said: "The writer is not 'one of the many.' Many do not seek the gallows for political freedom. However condemnable political murder may be, it is not possible to withhold recognition of the love of the country and the courage which inspires such awful deeds. And let us hope that the cult of political assassination is not growing if the Indian experiment succeeds, as it is bound to, the occupation of the political assassin will be gone for ever. At any rate, I am working in that faith."

"The writer does one less than justice when he says that I have made no more than sentimental appeals to the revolutionaries to call off their movement, and I claim on the contrary that I have given them hard facts which, though they have been often repeated in these columns, will bear recapitulation:

1. The revolutionary activity has not brought us near our goal.
2. It has added to the military expenditure in the country.
3. It has given rise to reprisals on the part of the government without doing any good.
4. Whenever a revolutionary murder has taken place, it has for a time and in that place demoralised the people.
5. It has in no way contributed to mass awakening.
6. Its effect on the masses has been doubly bad in that they tend to bear the burden ultimately of additional expense and the indirect effect of government wrath.

7. Revolutionary murder cannot thrive in the Indian soil, Indian tradition, as history teaches us, being unfavourable to the growth of political violence.

8. If the revolutionaries seek to convert the masses to their method, we would have to wait for an indefinitely long time for it to permeate the masses and then to gain freedom.

9. If the method of violence ever becomes popular, it is bound to recoil, as it has done in other countries, on our own heads.

10. The revolutionaries have an ocular demonstration of the efficacy of the opposite method, i.e., non-violence, which has gone on in spite of sporadic cases of violence on their part and in spite even of violence, occasionally dared by the so-called votaries of non-violence.

11. Revolutionaries should accept only testimony which tells them that their acitvity has not only not done any good to the movement of non-violence, but it has, on the contrary, harmed the cause. In other words, if I had a completely peaceful atmosphere, we would have gained our end already."

"These, I claim, are hard facts and no appeal to (sentence). But the writer further objects to my making public appeals to the party and suggests that thereby help the bureaucracy to crush the movement. Surely, the bureaucracy is in no need of my help to deal with the movement. It fights for life both against the revolutionary and me. One scents more danger from the non-violent movement than from the violent. It knows how to deal with the latter. It is baffled by the former which has already shaken it to its foundations."

"Moreover, authors of political murder count the cost before they enter upon their awful career. No action of mine can possibly worsen their fate. And seeing that the revolutionary party must work in secret, I have no other way open to me but that of making public appeals to its unknown members. I count many past revolutionaries among my co-workers."

"The open letter complains that prisoners other than satyagrahis have not been released. I have explained the reason why it was impossible to insist on the release of the other prisoners. Personally, I want the release of all of them. I would make every effort to secure their release. I am aware that some of them ought to have been discharged long ago. The Congress has a resolution in that behalf. Sjt. Nariman (a Congress leader) has been appointed by the Working Committee to collect all names. As soon as he has got the list, steps will be taken to secure their release. But those who are out must help by preventing revolutionary murder. We may not have the cake and also eat it. Of course, there are political prisoners, who should be discharged in any case. I can only give the assurance to all concerned that the delay is due not to want of will but due to want of ability. Let it be also remembered that when the final settlement comes, if it does, in the course of a few months, all political prisoners must be discharged. If it does not come, those who are trying to secure the release of the other political prisoners will find themselves in prison."

Epilogue

Awash with sunlight, Washington was bright and clean in November 1981. Even the cloistered chambers of Congressmen and Senators were bathed in light. But one room at 1088, Westside Drive had its curtains drawn as if the occupant preferred to live in the dark. But this was no surprise to the neighbours, who always found the shutters of the house down.

A few people remembered seeing the occupant who was tall, tense and abrupt in his behaviour. He shunned company. For the last several months he had confined himself to the room.

Old and drooping, Hans Raj Vohra liked to stay indoors all by himself. He was often drowned in thoughts. Why had he turned official approver against his comrades, the revolutionaries? He had been wanting to tell his side of the story for many years. But every time he felt like doing so, he decided to remain quiet. He had convinced himself that nobody would care to listen to his story. After all, his testimony was crucial to the death sentence given to three of his ex-comrades—Bhagat Singh, Sukhdev and Rajguru People would stay away from him when they heard who he was.

The way in which he was boycotted even by his friends after he turned approver had made him believe that he would be a social pariah. Even people closest to him had doubts about him. He had learnt to live with the odium. It had been a hard and lonely life but he had come to terms with it.

After the trial, the British whisked him off to the U.K. where he was admitted to London University. But for their help, he would not have got any job after the execution of Bhagat Singh and his two comrades. The first opening he had, after a stint in London, was with the English-owned newspaper, *Civil and Military Gazette*, in Lahore itself. A senior government official spoke to editor F.W. Bustin who hired him as a reporter. Even at that time Vohra had sensed that he would have to carry the stigma of betraying his friends and harming the revolutionaries' cause for the rest of his life.

He had never forgotten the contempt on Bhagat Singh's face when the two met each other at the magistrate's court. Sukhdev had recruited him to the party. But it was Bhagat Singh who became very close to him. Vohra too had once run away from his home to escape his father's scoldings on his association with the revolutionaries. Only Bhagat Singh's message made him return.

Was he to blame for the hanging of the three men? He had paid enough for the sins he told himself he had not committed. A few months before Partition, he had joined *The Statesman,* Calcutta, the daily owned by a British. Bustin had spoken to Editor Arthur Moore, who made him a special correspondent in Delhi.

The position gave him an opportunity to come in touch with senior politicians. But he always had a nagging feeling that they did not confide in him. His past always caught up with his future.

He took the first opportunity to get a posting abroad.*The Times of India* hired him as its Washington correspondent. After retirement he did not go back to India and became a representative of*Deccan Herald* in the US. Subsequently, he started his own feature service. The passage of time had dimmed the memory of Bhagat Singh's execution. But whenever his sacrifice was recalled, Vohra's name cropped up as the person who had given evidence against Bhagat Singh. Vohra had decided to spend the rest of his life in the US and die unknown.

A letter he received from India, 50 years after the hangings, shook Vohra. It was a letter from his old friend, Sukhdev's brother, Mathura Das Thapar, an engineer. Thapar reminded Vohra that posterity would like to know why he had let down his comrades.

Vohra had decided to die in America, unnoticed and unheard. The letter accused him of what he thought was not true. Thapar's insinuation was biting: "Why did you forget that foreign rulers of our country, in collusion with their administrative machinery, which included Indians, followed a policy of suppression of the people?"

Thapar still seemed to have faith in him. Sukhdev's brother reminded Vohra of the time when he stood firm even at the age of 17 after a bomb exploded at the Dussehra ground in Lahore in 1926. The authorities could not break him. Sukhdev had praised him then. Why then did he change when he was arrested in the Lahore Conspiracy Case, Thapar asked.

Thapar, whom Vohra called brother, had pointed a finger of blame at him. Vohra felt he must explain his side of the story. In any case, he did not have many days left to live. Doctors had diagnosed a malignant growth which was worsening because of heavy drinking. If it was a confession, it should be handwritten.

Vohra was a stickler for form. Even during the height of summer in Delhi, he wore a jacket with a necktie. He looked at the typewriter in the corner of his room for a long time. He could not decide whether he should type out his reply or write it in longhand. He felt that the keyboard left traces behind and so decided to write to Thapar in longhand.

In his letter, Vohra said: "I was moved by your letter and your overflowing affection which I do not in the least deserve. I regret we did not meet. In retrospect (who knows?) it was probably a good thing. If we had met, we would have talked of old times and what happened in the twenties when I was only 17 years old. I understand you have researched the episode very thoroughly. I have often thought of doing it myself and also about writing a book on it. But second thoughts have deterred me. Anything I wrote would be treated as biased and self-serving. It would be a waste of time, although I still believe a factual account would be a helpful contribution to the history of the period..."

"You have every right to be proud of Sukhdev. He was the soul of the party, a real organiser. I guess he is your hero. But I explained to Balbir (Vohra's cousin) how my views changed and what in fact happened. Probably he has conveyed my version of events to you. That is why I hold that our non-meeting was a good thing..."

"It has been a most difficult life, full of risks, but so far, touch-wood, I have emerged virtually unscathed at least physically. But the memory of the twenties accompanies me doggedly, teasingly, hauntingly, painingly. I have adopted a semi-public career as a journalist. I had to steer through the 44 years of a writing career like a fish in murky waters, seeking professional success while avoiding public recognition. It is amazing and extremely satisfying that, despite unavoidable handicaps, I have achieved the utmost professional success in my line of journalism."

"...I still earn my living purely by wielding my pen, which is a clean way to spend my remaining years particularly because my profession imbibes expression with thinking, art with craft and reading with writing. I hope by the time I die, I would have been fully forgotten. This is my ambition."

Thapar replied to Vohra's letter dated October 7, 1980 nearly a year later on September 9, 1981 and sought "elaboration and more information".

He said: "It gratified me to know that you have now achieved the utmost professional success in your line of journalism after having passed through a life of struggle and uncertainties... But, in the midst of those dulcet notes I also heard discordant ones: that in spite of utmost professional success, you have been avoiding public recognition, and that (to quote your own concluding words) 'I hope by the time I die I would have been fully forgotten. This is my only ambition'... Fatalism may be a piece of ill-advised philosophy where it leads to inaction, to an endless wait for the happy chance to fall from heavens above; but it is, without any reservations, commendable where merit and efforts, for one reason or the other, don't bear the desired fruit; it is a balm of all hurt minds. You seem to have yielded to self-mortification which, to my mind, is a temptation breeding ill-humour and which bedins life's serenity and sunshine."

"What in fact happened (to quote your own words) is my genuine curiosity to know. And, it is raised to such an extent that I may even make bold to ask that if you thought that Sukhdev yielded to weakness or some such thing when the conspiracy was unearthed, why you didn't remain firm as you had been on the earlier occasion, and why you have been harbouring an aversion for him when he, till his last, ever held you in esteem..."

Could Sukhdev have made a 'confession' to gain the confidence of the police? Vohra wondered. Sukhdev wanted access to comrade Jai Gopal, who had become an official approver. Sukhdev had chosen him as a messenger to inform Bhagat Singh, Rajguru and Azad about the arrival of Scott at his office. Jai Gopal identified Saunders as Scott. He was the police's key witness, who had witnessed the murder of Saunders. Did Sukhdev confess only to get close to Jaispal and kill him?

Vohra thought he would tell all. He said in the second letter: "My Guru (Sukhdev), I felt, had let me down. Together with the rest of the public, I could not go down with the people I no longer respected."

Below is Vohra's letter dated November 27, 1981, three months after Thapar's reply:

"Hans R.Vohra, Editor, US Feature Service

My dear Mathuradasji,

"I must ask your forgiveness for the delay in answering your affectionate letter.

"Your affection is so overwhelming and unexpected that I continue to be surprised by it for I prefer to label myself as a political leper. Perhaps this little poem would explain the situation:

> Once I had a friend,
> A leper friend was he
> Could you shake him by the hand,
> Chorus: Oh, No.
> Could you look him in the eye,
> Chorus: Oh, No.
> Could you sleep with him,
> Chorus: Oh No, No.
> That was the tragedy.

"I am not much of a poet, but I hope this stanza does explain my true feeling about myself. That is why I wonder whether you are not wasting your sentiments on a person consumed by grief over the turn his life has taken."

"As I have told you, it would be very inappropriate for me to talk about the Sukhdev case and the role he played after his arrest. I had the relevant chapter read to me. Since you compel me, I cannot in all honesty say that I agree with your conclusions."

"I shall deliberately confine this letter to my personal reactions to the events."

"I was arrested on the eve of Saunders' murder. This did not surprise me. I was the most important and the most well-known student leader in town. At the age of 17 or so, I became the first Secretary of the Punjab Students movement which I tried to convert into a public forum for our revolutionary movement."

"I called a Punjab Students conference which was astonishingly well attended. I proposed a resolution for complete independence for India when the Indian National Congress was comtemplating Dominion Status. So I put the students ahead of the elders.

"After my arrest, *the burden of concealing the murder conspiracy*, about which I knew everything, fell on my shoulders. When I was released on bail several weeks after the arrest, I had carried out my responsibility to the party successfully. The secret remained locked in my chest. I do not want to write about the ordeal in the police lockup lest you should construe that I am asking for mercy or that I am flattering myself."

"However, when I was arrested a second time, soon after the rounding up of Sukhdev and some other party members, I was presented a statement by Sukhdev which ran, I believe, into probably 100 or (50) pages, typewritten and foolscap."

"Secondly, I found that about eight or ten members of the party, and every senior members at that, had become the King's witnesses or approvers as (they) call them."

So I had to think things anew in the light of the following facts: "Sukhdev at whose command I had given up my family and whom I had accepted as my guru had wrecked the party which he had done so much to create."

"It was an inexplicable situation, totally disappointing and terribly shattering of moral or the common purpose we had set out to serve."

"I cannot accept your explanation that he became nervous (*ghabra gaya*). This is so inadequate for a would-be hero of a story that it mocks his better side. He was a great organiser. He was selflessly devoted to the cause. He was a ceaseless worker. He was a convincing talker which is apparent as I joined the party at his behest."

"To this day, I do not know what precisely went through his mind that he burst like a Diwali balloon within hours of being arrested. I am absolutely sure that the police did not use any high-handed methods. If anything, the investigators were very respectful and kind."

"Sukhdev voluntarily divulged every secret of the party. There was nothing important to keep although I did find a few things which he had forgotten to mention and which, therefore, I also withheld in my statement."

"Sukhdev's performance presents two problems, none of which you have solved; (a) if he had no axe to grind, why did he make the statement?; (b) having made the statement why did he not take some advantage from it?"

"As I have said, there is no rational reason for (a) except that his mind was like a tumbler of water. The tumbler cracked and the water overflowed."

"Having thus mentally evacuated himself, I guess, he was at peace. But his overflowing knowledge about the party, which he freely cast away, created problems for others. Mine has remained my companion throughout my life."

"My life is stunted and stained and there is nothing I can do to wash away the horrible marks so deeply etched in history."

"I gave up the resistance to the investigating police for the following reasons: (a) My guru, I felt, had let me down together with the rest of the party. My portion of the story was relatively small and inconsequential as compared with what had been given away."

"I was consumed by helplessness and although it is easy to say that I would have received a light punishment, I could not risk going down with people I no longer respected."

"Secondly, it would have meant a total disruption of my life as I was in my final year of education."

"So I tried very deftly, without doing the least possible additional harm to the party, to extricate myself so that I could pick up the remaining pieces as best as I could."

"(1) I was able to abstain from giving any personal evidence of the murder, which I had seen organised and which I had seen being readied a few minutes before the execution."

"I said nothing about it. So I was neither a witness to the conspiracy of the murder nor of the murder."

"(2) I also take such credit as I can for abstaining to mention anything about Durga Das whom I had recruited."

"I was able to do both because I found that Sukhdev's statement had omitted them."

"You must also remember that I was the youngest member of the party. But I did understand the legal consequences of actions. Even while giving evidence, I tried to do the least harm, and possibly some good as Durga Das has often acknowledged to me."

"I would be grateful if you give copies of our correspondence to Balbir as he is interested in the case."

"Once again, I must seek your pardon if I have unwittingly written anything derogatory of Sukhdev. You have every reason to treat him as a hero. He was your brother. I have written this letter about my experience of the case much against my wishes."

With kind regards,

Yours affectionately,
(H.R.Vohra)

Thapar took nearly five months to reply to Vohra's letter. It was a long 14-page reply typed in single space (See Annexure IV).

Thapar summarised Vohra's reply— "Your grudge," as he put it into four points: "(1) That after your third and the last arrest on May,1929, you were shown about a hungred-page statement (alleged to have been made) by Sukhdev; (2) that Sukhdev being an important leader, let you and others down, and destroyed the party which he so much harboured to create; (3) that eight or 10 senior members of the party had become King's witnesses; and (4) you wondered that, having made the statement, why Sukhdev did not take advantage unto himself. "

Thapar argued that the statement "which was shown to you was concocted by the police…" He contradicted Vohra's allegation that the Punjab police did not use any high-handed methods against Sukhdev. Thapar said "that the police had resorted to third degree methods in trying to break him and bend him. But his spirits remained undaunted and firm in resolve, though his body bore marks of cruelty…" Now, what actually happened was that Jai Gopal's statement must have upset Sukhdev. As soon as he came to know of it, he told the investigating police that instead of demanding from Jai Gopal, they should better ask him for details, he being in the know of every thing as an important leader. In assuming this posture, which caused much misunderstanding in the minds of his associates, Sukhdev's purpose was to, somehow take the police into confidence and gain their favour so that he could get access to Jai Gopal in order to strangle him to death. This was what Sukhdev confessed to some of us of the family when we met him while he was in the custody of Aziz Ahmad, who was In-Charge of the Conspiracy Case, and Sardar Gopa, Singh, Deputy Superintendent.

Thapar alleged that Yashpal, the Hindi writer, was a police informer. "He used to gather all information from Jai Gopal and then pass it on to the police. Though now dead a few years, he is fondly remembered by his admirers as a great revolutionary and a Hindi writer of no mean significance." What an irony!

In his reply dated October 9, 1982, Vohra said: "I cannot for the life of me agree that Sukhdev's actions after arrest were guided by the motive you have attributed. It is too fantastic to be credible. Nor can I accept the thesis that his long statement was a police concoction. This is at variance with his effort to guide the police to some of the party's hideouts even if he did not show all of them. Nor did I find any substance in your assumption of torture by the police who used the more powerful weapon of politeness, respect and indulgence."

Vohra concluded the correspondence by saying: "The best thing we can do is to agree amiably to disagree or that we can meet in a friendly way when I visit India in December." He never returned to his country.

Thapar too closed the correspondence by writing on November 19, 1982: "Yes, there seems to be cleavage in our views which, as you say, cannot be closed. Hence it would be proper if we do no more talking on this affair."

"How to check Vohra's version?" I asked myself. Thapar could not say anything beyond what the letter said when I sought more information from him. He died before I could meet him. He did not publicise Vohra's letter as if he did not believe him. But Thapar was fair: he sent Vohra's letter to his family members in New Delhi.

One person, Durga Devi, widow of Bhagwati Charan, Bhagat Singh's close associate, should have known the truth. I checked with her. She was living in Ghaziabad with her son Sachin when I met her. She suffered from frequent memory lapses. But she recalled Vohra whom she dismissed as "a small functionary in the party". Regarding Vohra's allegation, she said: "We suspected Sukhdev all along."

Still suspicion cannot change the facts. Sukhdev was hanged along with Bhagat Singh and Rajguru. There is no evidence that he faltered during the trial or later. He was as defiant as he was in school when he was caned because he had refused to salute visiting white military officers. If he was the person who divulged everything to the police, why was he not pardoned in place of Vohra? Sukhdev had far more knowledge than Vohra.

Vohra probably fell prey to the usual tactics of the police. Even today the ruse employed by them is: "Your comrade has already spilled the beans. You may as well tell your side and we would try to get you pardon." Something like that might have happend. In any case, Vohra's role is not convincing. How could a person with even a grain of commitment to revolution turn into a stool-pigoen?

Vohra must have recalled the time when his involvement was not even questioned. Wherever and whenever the revolutionaries wanted him, he was there. He was not a Marxist. But the thought of emancipation from the British animated him. He was present at every closed-door meeting and not once did he give the impression of being a person who had second thoughts on joining the ranks of the revolutionaries.

Vohra died on September 13, 1985, in his room in Washington, with the shutters down. He could keep the light out but not the darkness. He was cremated in Washington before a clutch of his family members.

The difference between Sukhdev and Vohra is underlined by people's response. The ashes of Bhagat Singh, Sukhdev and Rajguru were consigned to a shrine near Ferozepur where thousands of people flock to pay their homage even today. The crematorium where Vohra's body was put to fire is not even known. Sukhdev is a hero.

Annexure - I

Mr. Kuldip Nayar,
D-7/2,Vasant Vihar,
New Delhi-1100567.

My dear Mr. Nayar,

I am in receipt of your letter of 22nd October, 1992 and am sorry for the delay in reply. Many factors are responsible for the delay including my failing health — being 82 years old and having eye trouble requiring operation of both the eyes. Besides failing physical health I am without a proper shelter after retirement as cold storage expert. I have worked in such an organisation in Hapur since 1940. Before this I was in Saharanpur from 1936 to 1940 in a ice factory of L.,Ram Labhaya Chanaan of Lyallpur, one amongst the family of old Congress politicians of Punjab. The reason I came away from Lyallpur was due to the constant troubles created against me by the Punjab Police on account of my being the blood brother of Sukhdev—the BRAIN BEHIND THE CONSPIRACY as per the notings of the British Police Officer in Punjab Police, the TRIO combine of Sukhdev, Bhagat Singh and Rajguru. I always acted like a carrier of letters exchanged by the head of the conspirators named above (Sukhdev)—letter by Sukhdev to Mahatma Gandhi—that he wrote just before being HANGED on 23rd March, 1931. No one from amongst the Congress leaders of Punjab cared to accept the letter to be carried to Karachi Congress Session held there by 31st March, 1931 (sic). L. Chint Ram, our uncle, a very big Congress leader of Punjab could not go as he was to reach Lyallpur to be present there to sit as the HEAD of the Thapar clan to receive the mourners who were to reach Lyallpur to mourn the sad end of Sukhdev. L.Pindi Das and other Congress leaders heading for the Karachi Session refused to carry the letter to Mahatma Gandhi for the fear of being REBUKED and branded by the Mahatama as hand in glove with conspirator to indicate any kind of link or association with the above TERRORISTS. I was therefore asked by L. Chint Ram—our uncle and HEAD OF THE THAPAR clan, to proceed to Karachi to carry the letter to be delivered to Gandhiji. I reached by the train carrying the Congress leaders to Karachi and in spite of all the beating and insulting offensive attitude of Congress volunteers, I could after all meet the P.A. to Gandhiji's, Shri Mahadev Desai, and delivered the letter. Gandhiji being awfully busy at that very important session after the HANGING of the THREE HEROES, Mr. Desai told me to CONVEY IT TO L. CHINT RAM that the letter will be replied by Gandhi Jee only after the session and its reply can be seen in Navjivan (Hindi) and Young India (English) after Gandhi Jee returns to Wardha.

Before this also I was twice jailed in the years 1927-28 and 1930-31, once when Sukhdev wrote a letter addressed to 'BIRATHER-AE-MUN' and was to be posted at my address in Lahore; and before that in Lyallpur when a BOMB exploded in Company Bagh Club of the British officers. Many others were arrested in Lyallpur but they were all let off but I was held for being the nephew of L. Chint Ram and the real younger brother of SUKHDEV and imprisoned for FOUR MONTHS in Qilla Gujar Singh, Lahore. It will not be out of place to add that I suffered most when my brother was in the process of writing the above entitled letter to my address in Lahore, which my brother wrote from BORSTAL JAIL, Lahore. This he did after he was condemned along with others (Bhagat Singh and Rajguru). Immediately Police rushed to Borstal Jail and snatched the letter that was half finished and Aziz Ahmed, the head of police party questioned SUKHDEV as to whom this letter was to be sent. He said this is for my comrades–other party KRANTIKARIES WHOSE NAME HE refused to disclose. He (AZIZ AHMED) then told him that under the circumstances your brother Mathura Das Thapar will be taken into custody and jailed and suffer police torture. He replied, "so what, he has been always suffering from Police Excesses in the past as well" "and will once again face the police torture. But under no circumstances the names of his comrades will be disclosed to whom this letter was meant." The Police party had gone to Borstal Jail to transfer him to Central Jail to be lodged in the cell meant for condemned convicts. The death sentence had just been passed and all condemned were transferred immediately to Central Jail cells meant for housing the condemned.

I was again under the GRIP of Punjab Police and suffered jail torture for many months to come.

Allow me the indulgence to add further that other Political sufferers like Dr.Kitchloo's son got a monthly packet of Rs.5000-00 plus a lump sum compensation of Rs.50,000-00 and also a DDA flat free of cost. As compared to Dr.Kitchloo's son compare our Clan's sacrifices—L.Chint Ram suffered (my uncle went to Jail several times from 1907 onwards in the struggle for FREEDOM of the country and my elder brother was hanged along with Bhagat Singh and Rajguru and I was also a victim of Police torture repeatedly and this was the main reason, I moved out of Punjab at the advice of our Uncle L. Chint Ram as said above.

Now coming to the main point about the material for your proposed book on BHAGAT SINGH TRIAL, I may again draw your kind attention to PROCEEDINGS BOOK of LAHORE CONSPIRACY CASE, that I have presented to the National Archives in New Delhi. This is the only document I had compiled which runs into more than 400 pages. I may tell you that I collected the entire case documents from Lahore High Court and other relevant documents that in itself are the HISTORY of National Importance. The case—the Lahore Conspiracy Case reads in Govt. records as "SUKHDEV VS KING AND OTHER ACCUSED." The English version and the judgement in English, comprising of the "PROCEEDINGS BOOK" are in the National Archives and its version in Urdu in three volumes is with me. I have also many more documents of interest to a WORLD FAME writer like your goodself. I can place at your disposal for some time all these documents in my possession that I have collected from Lahore High Court by spending time and money to obtain these records. Please note that as and when I go to Delhi I stay with my daughter Mrs.Lata Gujral at No.L-15, First Floor, South Extension, Part (II), New Delhi. They are on telephone and shall give you the telephone number later if you feel further interested to have a look at the other relative papers and documentary proof available with me.

With best regards and hoping to be of use in your GREAT TASK of writing another masterpiece of great HISTORIC IMPORTANCE.

Sincerely Yours,
Sd/-
(M.D.Thapar)

Annexure-II

Why I am an Atheist

A NEW QUESTION HAS CROPPED UP, IS IT DUE TO vanity that I do not believe in the existence of an omnipotent, omnipresent and omniscient God? I had never imagined that I would ever have to confront such a question. But conversation with some friends has given me a hint that certain of my friends—if I am not claiming too much in thinking them to be so—are inclined to conclude from the brief contact they have had with me, that it was too much on my part to deny the existence of God and that there was a certain amount of vanity that actuated my disbelief. Well, the problem is a serious one. I do not boast to be quite above these human traits. I am a man and nothing more. None can claim to be more. I also have this weakness in me. Vanity does form a part of my nature. Amongst my comrades I was called an autocrat. Even my friend Mr.B.K.Dutt sometimes called me so. On certain occasions I was decried as a despot. Some friends do complain, and very seriously too, that I involuntarily thrust my opinions upon others and get my proposals accepted. That this is true up to a certain extent, I do not deny. This may amount to egotism. There is vanity in me inasmuch as our cult as opposed to other popular creeds is concerned. But that is not personal. It may be, it is only legitimate pride in our cult and does not amount to vanity. Vanity, or to be more precise "Ahankar" is the excess of undue pride in one's self. Whether it is such an undue pride that has led me to atheism or whether it is after very careful study of the subject and after much consideration that I have come to disbelieve in God, is a question that I intend to discuss here. Let me first make it clear that egotism and vanity are two different things.

In the first place, I have altogether failed to comprehend as to how undue pride or vaingloriousness could ever stand in the way of a man in believing in God. I can refuse to recognise the greatness of a really great man, provided, I have also achieved a certain amount of popularity without deserving it or without having possessed the qualities really essential or indispensable for the same purpose. That much is conceivable. But in what way can a man believing in God cease believing due to his personal vanity? There are only two ways. The man should either begin to think himself a rival of God or he may begin to believe himself to be a God. In neither case, can he become a genuine atheist. In the first case he does not even deny the existence of his rival. In the second case as well, he admits the existence of a conscious being behind the screen guiding all the movements of nature. It is of no importance to us whether he thinks himself to be that supreme being or · whether he thinks the supreme conscious being to be somebody apart from himself. The fundamental is there. His belief is there. He is by no means an atheist. Well, here I am. I neither belong to the first category nor to the second. I deny the very existence of that Almighty Supreme Being. Why I deny it, shall be dealt with later on. Here I want to clear one thing, that it is not vanity that has actuated me to adopt the doctrines of atheism. I am neither a rival nor an incarnation, nor the Supreme Being Himself. One point is decided, that it is not vanity that has led me to this mode of thinking. Let me examine the facts to disprove this allegation. According to these friends of mine, I have grown vainglorious perhaps due to the undue popularity gained during the trials— both Delhi Bomb and Lahore Conspiracy Cases. Well, let us see if their premises are correct. My atheism is not of so recent origin. I had stopped believing in God when I was an obscure young man, of whose existence my above-mentioned friends were not even aware. At least a college student cannot cherish any short of undue pride which may lead him to atheism. Though a favourite with some professors and disliked by certain others. I was never an industrious or a studious boy. I could not get any chance of indulging in such feelings as vanity. I was rather a boy with a very shy nature, who had certain pessimistic dispositions about the future career. And in those days, I was not a perfect atheist. My grandfather under whose influence I was brought up is an orthodox Arya Samajist. An Arya Samajist is anything but an atheist. After finishing my primary education I joined the D.A.V. School of Lahore and stayed in its Boarding House for full one year. There, apart from morning and evening prayers, I used to recite "Gayatri Mantra" for hours and hours. I was a perfect devotee in those days. Later on I began to live with my father. He is a liberal in as much as the orthodoxy of religions is concerned. It was through his teachings that I aspired to devote my life to the cause of freedom. But he is not an atheist. He is a firm believer. He used to encourage me for offering prayers daily. So this is how I was brought up. In the Non-Cooperation days I joined the National College. It was there that I began to think liberally and discuss and criticise all the religious problems, even about God. But still I was a devout believer. By that time I had begun to preserve the unshorn and unclipped long hair but I could never believe in the mythology and doctrines of Sikhism or any other religion. But I had a firm faith in God's existence.

Later on I joined the revolutionary party. The first leader with whom I came in contact, though not convinced, could not dare to deny the existence of God. On my persistent inquiries about God, he used to say: "Pray whenever you want to." Now this is atheism less courage required for the adoption of that creed. The second leader with whom I came in contact was a firm believer. Let me mention his name—respected Comrade Shachindra Nath Sanyal, now undergoing life transportation in connection with the Kakori Conspiracy Case. From the very first page of his famous and only book, Bandi Jivan (or Incarcerated Life), the Glory of God is sung vehemently. On the last page of the second part of that beautiful book, his mystic—because of vedantism—praises showered upon God form a very conspicuous part of his thoughts. "The Revolutionary leaflet" distributed throughout India on January 28th, 1925, was, according to the prosecution story, the result of his intellectual labour. Now, as is inevitable in the secret work, the prominent leader expresses his own views which are very dear to his person, and the rest of the workers have to acquiesce in them, in spite of differences which they might have. In that leaflet one full paragraph was devoted to praise the Almighty and His rejoicing and doings. That is all mysticism. What I wanted to point out was that the idea of disbelief had not even germinated in the revolutionary party. The famous Kakori martyrs—all four of them passed their last days in prayers. Ram Prasad Bismil was an orthodox Arya Samajist. Despite his wide studies in the field of socialism and communism, Rajen Lahiri could not suppress his desire of reciting hymns of the Upanishads and the Gita. I saw only one man amongst them, who never prayed and used to say:

"Philosophy is the outcome of human weakness or limitation of knowledge." He is also undergoing a sentence of transportation for life. But he also never dared to deny the existence of God.

Up to that period I was only a romantic idealist revolutionary. Up till then we were to follow. Now came the time to shoulder the whole responsibility. Due to the inevitable reaction for some time the very existence of the party seemed impossible. Enthusiastic comrades- nay, leaders- began to jeer at us. For some time I was afraid that some day I also might not be convinced of the futility of our own programme. That was a turning point in my revolutionary career. "Study" was the cry that reverberated in the corridors of my mind. Study to enable yourself to face the arguments advanced by opposition. Study to arm yourself with arguments in favour of your cult. I began to study. My previous faith and convictions underwent a remarkable modification. The romance of the violent methods alone which was so prominent amongst our predecessors, was replaced by serious ideas. No more mysticism, no more blind faith. Realism became our cult. Use of force justifiable when resorted to as a matter of terrible necessity: non-violence as policy indispensable for all mass movements. So much about methods. The most important thing was the clear conception of the ideal for which we were to fight. As there were no important activities in the field of action I got ample opportunity to study various ideals of the world revolution. I studied Bakunin, the anarchist leader, something of Marx, the father of communism, and much of Lenin, Trotsky and others—the men who had successfully carried out a revolution in their country. They were all atheists. Bakunin's God and State, though only fragmentary, is an interesting study of the subject. Later still I came across a book entitled Common Sense by Nirlamba Swami. It was only a sort of mystic atheism. This subject became of utmost interest to me. By the end of 1926 I had been convinced as to the baselessness of the theory of existence of an almighty supreme being who created, guided and controlled the universe. I had given out this disbelief of mine. I began discussion on the subject with my friends. I had become a pronounced atheist. But what it meant will presently be discussed.

In May 1927 I was arrested at Lahore. The arrest was a surprise. I was quite unaware of the fact that the police wanted me. All of a sudden, while passing through a garden, I found myself surrounded by police. To my own surprise, I was very calm at that time. I did not feel any sensation, nor did I experience any excitement. I was taken into police custody. Next day I was taken to the Railway Police lock-up where I was to pass full one month. After many day's conversation with the police officials I guessed that they had some information regarding my connection with the Kakori party and my other activities in connection with the revolutionary movement. They told me that I had been to Lucknow while the trial was going on there, that I had negotiated a certain scheme about their rescue, that after obtaining their approval, we had procured some bombs, that by way of test one of·the bombs was thrown in the crowd on the occasion of Dussehra 1926. They further informed me, in my interest, that if I could give any statement throwing some light on the activities of the revolutionary party, I was not to be imprisoned but on the contrary set free and rewarded, even without being produced as an approver in the court. I laughed at the proposal. It was all humbug. People holding ideas like ours do not throw bombs on their own innocent people. One fine morning Mr.Newman, the then Senior Superintendent of C.I.D., came to me. And after much sympathetic talk with me, imparted- to him the extremely sad-news that if I did not give any statement as demanded by them, they would be forced to send me up for trial for conspiracy to wage war in connection with Kakori Case and for brutal murders in connection with Dussehra bomb outrage. And he further informed me that they had evidence enough to get me convicted and hanged. In those days I believed— though I was quite innocent—the police could do it if they desired. That very day certain police officials began to persuade me to offer my prayers to God regularly, both the times. Now I was an atheist. I wanted to settle for myself whether it was in the days of peace and enjoyment alone that I could boast of being an atheist or whether during such hard times as well, I could stick to those principles of mine. After great consideration I decided that I could not lead myself to believe in and pray to God. No, I never did. That was the real test and I came out successful. Never for a moment did I desire to save my neck at the cost of certain other things. So I was a staunch disbeliever; and have ever since been. It was not an easy job to stand that test. 'Belief' softens the hardships, even can make them pleasant. In God man can find very strong consolation and support. Without Him man has to depend upon himself. To stand upon one's own legs amid storms and hurricanes is not a child's play. At such testing moments, vanity—if any—evaporates, and man cannot dare to defy the general beliefs. If he does, then we must conclude that he has got certain other strength than mere vanity. This is exactly the situation now. Judgement is already too well known. Within a week it is to be pronounced. What is the consolation with the exception of the idea that I am going to sacrifice my life for a cause? A God-believing Hindu might be expecting to be reborn as a king, a Muslim or a Christian might dream of the luxuries to be enjoyed in paradise and the reward he is to get for his suffering and sacrifices. But, what am I to expect? I know the moment the rope is fitted round my neck and rafters removed from under my feet, that will be the final moment—that will be the last moment. I, or to be more precise, my soul as interpreted in the metaphysical terminology shall all be finished there. Nothing further. A short life of struggle with no such magnificent end, shall in itself be the reward, if I have the courage to take it in that light. That is all. With no selfish motive or desire to be awarded here or hereafter, quite disinterestedly, have I devoted my life to the cause of independence, because I could not do otherwise. The day we find a great number of men and women with this psychology, who cannot devote themselves to anything else than the service of mankind and emancipation of the suffering humanity, that day shall inaugurate the era of liberty. Not to become a king, nor to gain any other rewards here, or in the next birth or after death in paradise, shall they be inspired to challenge the oppressors, exploiters, and tyrants, but to cast off the yoke of serfdom from the neck of humanity and to establish liberty and peace shall they tread this- to their individual selves perilous and to their noble selves the only glorious imaginable- path. Is the pride in their noble cause to be misinterpreted as vanity? Who dares to utter such an abominable epithet? To him I say either he is a fool or a knave. Let us forgive him for he cannot realise the depth, the emotion, the sentiment and the noble feelings that surge in that heart. His heart is dead as a mere lump of flesh, his eyes are weak, the evils of other interests having been cast over them. Self-reliance is always liable to be interpreted as vanity. It is sad and miserable but there is no help.

You go and oppose the prevailing faith, you go and criticise a hero, a great man who is generally believed to be above criticism because he is thought to be infallible, the strength of your argument shall force the multitude to decry you as vainglorious. This is due to the mental stagnation. Criticism and independent thinking are the two indispensable qualities of a revolutionary. Because Mahatmaji is great, therefore none should criticise him. Because he has risen above, therefore everything he says—may be in the field of Politics or Religion, Economics or Ethics—is right. Whether you are convinced or not you must say: "Yes, that's true". This mentality does not lead towards progress. It is rather too obviously reactionary.

Because our forefathers had set up a faith in some supreme being—the Almighty God—therefore, any man who dares to challenge the validity of that faith, or the very existence of that supreme being, he shall have to be called an apostate, a renegade. If his arguments are too sound to be refuted by counter-arguments and spirit too strong to be cowed down by the threat of misfortunes that may befall him by the wrath of the Almighty, he shall be decried as vainglorious, his spirit to be denominated as vanity. Then, why to waste time in this vain discussion? Why try to argue out the whole thing? This question is coming before the public for the first time, and is being handled in this matter of fact way for the first time, hence this lengthy discussion.

As for the first question, I think I have cleared that it is not vanity that has led me to atheism. My way of argument has proved to be convincing or not, that is to be judged by my readers, not me. I know in the present circumstances my faith in God would have made my life easier, my burden lighter, and my disbelief in Him has turned all the circumstances too dry, and the situation may assume too harsh a shape. A little bit of mysticism can make it poetical. But I do not want the help of any intoxication to meet my fate. I am a realist. I have been trying to overpower the instinct in me by the help of reason. I have not always been successful in achieving this end. But man's duty is to try and endeavour, success depends upon chance and environments.

As for the second question that if it was not vanity, then there ought to be some reason to disbelieve the old and still prevailing faith in the existence of God. Yes, I come to that now. Reason there is. According to me, any man who has got some reasoning power at his command always tries to reason out his environments. Where direct proofs are lacking philosophy occupies the important place.

As I have already stated, a certain revolutionary friend used to say that philosophy is the outcome of human weakness. When our ancestors had leisure enough to try to solve out the mystery of this world, its past, present and the future, its whys and wherefores, they having been terribly short of direct proofs, everybody tried to solve the problem in his own way. Hence we find the wide differences in the fundamentals of various religious creeds, which sometimes assume very antagonistic and conflicting shapes. Not only the Oriental and occidental philosophies differ, there are differences even amongst various schools of thought in each hemisphere. Amongst Oriental religions, the Moslem faith is not at all compatible with Hindu faith. In India alone Buddhism and Jainism are sometimes quite separate from Brahmanism, in which there are again conflicting faiths as Arya Samaj and Sanatan Dharma. Charwak is still another independent thinker of the past ages. He challenged the authority of God in the old times. All these creeds differ from each other on the fundamental question; and everybody considers himself to be on the right. There lies the misfortune. Instead of using the experiments and expressions of the ancient Savants and thinkers as a basis for our future struggle against ignorance and to try to find out a solution to this mysterious problem, we, lethargical as we have proved to be, raise the hue and cry of faith, unflinching and unwavering faith to their versions and thus are guilty of stagnation in human progress.

Any man who stands for progress has to criticise, disbelieve and challenge every item of the old faith. Item by item he has to reason out every nook and corner of the prevailing faith. If after considerable reasoning one is led to believe in any theory or philosophy, his faith is welcomed. His reasoning can be mistaken, wrong, misled, and sometimes fallacious. But he is liable to correction because reason is the guiding star of his life. But mere faith and blind faith is dangerous: it dulls the brain, and makes a man reactionary. A man who claims to be a realist has to challenge the whole of the ancient faith. If it does not stand the onslaught of reason it crumbles down. Then the first thing for him is to shatter the whole down and clear a space for the erection of a new philosophy. This is the negative side. After it begins the positive work in which sometimes some material of the old faith may be used for the purpose of reconstruction. As far as I am concerned, let me admit at the very outset that I have not been able to study

much on this point. I had a great desire to study the Oriental
philosophy but I could not get any chance or opportunity to do the
same. But so far as the negative study is under discussion, I think
I am convinced to the extent of questioning the soundness of the old
faith. I have been convinced as to non-existence of a conscious
supreme being who is guiding and directing the movements of
nature. We believe in nature and the whole progressive movement
aims at the domination of man over nature for his service. There is
no conscious power behind it to direct. This is what our philosophy
is.

As far the negative side, we ask a few questions from the
'believers'.

(1) If, as you believe, there is an almighty, omnipresent,
omniscient and omnipotent God, who created the earth or world,
please let me know why did he create it? This world of woes and
miseries, a veritable, eternal combination of numberless tragedies:
Not a single soul being perfectly satisfied.

Pray, don't say that it is His Law. If he is bound by any law, he
is not omnipotent. He is another slave like ourselves. Please don't
say that it is his enjoyment. Nero burnt one Rome. He killed a very
limited number of people. He created very few tragedies, all to his
perfect enjoyment. And, what is his place in History? By what
names do the historians mention him? All the venomous epithets
are showered upon him. Pages are blackened with invective
diatribes condemning Nero, the tyrant, the heartless, the wicked.
One Changez Khan sacrificed a few thousand lives to seek pleasure
in it and we hate the very name. Then, how are you going to justify
your almighty, eternal Nero, who has been, and is still causing
numberless tragedies every day, every hour and every minute?
How do you think to support his misdoings which surpass those
of Changez every single moment? I say why did he create this
world—a veritable hell, a place of constant and bitter unrest? Why
did the Almighty create man when he had the power not to do it?
What is the justification for all this? Do you say, to award the
innocent sufferers hereafter and to punish the wrongdoers as dare
to inflict wounds upon your body to apply a very soft and soothing
ointment upon it afterwards? How far the supporters and
organisers of the Gladiator institution were justified in throwing
men before the half-starved furious lions to be cared for and well
looked after if they could survive and could manage to escape

death by the wild beasts? That is why I ask: Why did the conscious supreme being create this world and man in it? To seek pleasure? Where, then, is the difference between him and Nero?

You Mohammadans and Christians: Hindu philosophy shall still linger on to offer another argument. I ask you, what is your answer to the above-mentioned question? You don't believe in previous birth. Like Hindus, you cannot advance the argument of previous misdoings of the apparently quite innocent sufferers. I ask you, why did the omnipotent labour for six days to create the world through word and each day to say that all was well? Call him today. Show him the past history. Make him study the present situation. Let us see if he dares to say:"All is well".

From the dungeons of prisons, from stores of starvation consuming millions upon millions of human beings in slums and huts, from the exploited labourers, patiently or say apathetically watching the procedure of their blood being sucked by the capitalist vampires, and the wastage of human energy that will make a man with the least common sense shiver with horror, and from the preference of throwing the surplus of production in oceans rather than to distribute amongst the needy producers- to the places of kings built upon the foundation laid with human bones... let him see all this and let him say: "All is well." Why and wherefore? That is my question. You are silent. All right then, I proceed.

Well, you Hindus, you say all the present sufferers belong to the class of sinners of the previous births. Good. You say the present oppressors were sainty people in their previous births, hence they enjoy power. Let me admit that your ancestors were very shrewd people, they tried to find out theories strong enough to hammer down all the efforts of reason and disbelief. But let us analyse how far this argument can really stand.

From the point of view of the most famous jurists, punishment can be justified only from three or four ends, to meet which it is inflicted upon the wrongdoer. They are retributive, reformative and deterrent. The retributive theory is now being condemned by all the advanced thinkers. Deterrent theory is also following the same fate. Reformative theory is the only one which is essential and indispensable for human progress. It aims at returning the offender as a most competent and a peace-loving citizen to the society. But what is the nature of punishment inflicted by God upon men, even if we suppose them to be offenders? You say he sends them to be born as a cow, a cat, a tree, a herb or a beast. You enumerate these punishments to be 84 lakhs. I ask you: what is its reformative effect upon man? How many men have met you who say that they were born as a donkey in previous birth for having committed any sin? None.Don't quote your Puranas. I have no scope to touch your mythologies. Moreover, do you know that the greatest sin in this world is to be poor? Poverty is a sin, it is a punishment. I ask you how far would you appreciate a criminologist, a jurist or a legislator who proposes such measures of punishment which shall inevitably force men to commit more offences? Had not your God thought of this, or he also had to learn these things by experience, but at the cost of untold sufferings to be borne by humanity? What do you think shall be the fate of a man who has been born in a poor and illiterate family of, say, a chamar or a sweeper? He is poor, hence he cannot study. He is hated and shunned by his fellow human beings who think themselves to be his superiors having been born in say, a higher caste. His ignorance, his poverty and the treatment meted out to him shall harden his heart towards society. Suppose he commits a sin, who shall bear the consequences? God, he or the learned ones of the society? What about the punishment of those people who were deliberately kept ignorant by the haughty and egotist Brahmans, and who had to pay the penalty by bearing the stream of being led (not lead) in their ears for having heard a few sentences of your Sacred Books of learning—the Vedas? If they committed any offence, who was to be responsible for them and who was to bear the brunt? My dear friends, these theories are the inventions of the privileged ones; they justify their usurped power, riches and superiority by the help of these theories. Yes, it was perhaps Upton Sinclair that wrote at some place that just make a man a believer in immortality and then rob him of all his riches and possessions. He shall help you even in that ungrudgingly. The coalition among the religious preachers and possessors of power brought forth jails, gallows, knots and these theories.

Annexure-III

The Philosophy of the Bomb

RECENT EVENTS, PARTICULARLY THE CONGRESS resolution on the attempt to blow up the Viceregal Special on the 23 December,1929, and Gandhi's subsequent writings in Young India, clearly show that the Indian National Congress, in conjunction with Gandhi, has launched a crusade against the revolutionaries. A great amount of public criticism, both from the press and the platform, has been made against them. It is a pity that they have all along been, either deliberately or due to sheer ignorance, misrepresented and misunderstood. The revolutionaries do not shun criticism and public scrutiny of their ideals or actions. They rather welcome these as chances of making those understand, who have a genuine desire to do so, the basic principles of the revolutionary movement and the high and noble ideals that are a perennial source of inspiration and strength to it. It is hoped that this article will help the general public to know the revolutionaries as they are and will prevent it from taking them for what interested and ignorant persons would have it believe them to be.

VIOLENCE OR NON-VIOLENCE

LET US, first of all, take up the question of violence and non-violence. We think that the use of these terms in itself, is a grave injustice to either party, for they express the ideals of neither of them correctly. Violence is physical force applied for committing injustice, and that is certainly not what the revolutionaries stand for. On the other hand, what generally goes by the name of non-violence is in reality the theory of soul force, as applied to the attainment of personal and national rights through courting, suffering and hoping thus to finally convert your opponent to your point of view. When a revolutionary believes certain things to be his right he asks for them, pleads for them, argues for them, wills to attain them with all the soul-force at his command, stands the greatest amount of suffering for them, is always prepared to make the highest sacrifice for their attainment, and also backs his efforts with all the physical force he is capable of. You may coin what other word you like to describe his methods but you cannot call it violence, because that would constitute an outrage on the dictionary meaning of that word. Satyagraha is insistence upon truth. Why press, for the acceptance of truth, by soul-force alone? Why not add physical force also to it? While the revolutionaries stand for winning independence by all the forces, physical as well as moral, at their command, the advocates of soul-force would like to ban the use of physical force. The question really, therefore, is not whether you will have violence, but whether you will have soul-force plus physical force or soul-force alone.

OUR IDEAL

THE REVOLUTIONARIES believe that the deliverance of their country will come through revolution. The revolution, they are constantly working and hoping for, will not only express itself in the form of an armed conflict between the foreign government and its supporters and the people, it will also usher in a new social order. The revolution will ring the death knell of capitalism and class distinctions and privileges. It will bring joy and prosperity to the starving millions who are seething today under the terrible yoke of both foreign and Indian exploitation. It will bring the nation into its own. It will give birth to a new state—a new social order. Above all, it will establish the dictatorship of the proletariat and will for ever banish social parasites from the seat of political power.

TERRORISM

THE REVOLUTIONARIES already see the advent of the revolution in the restlessness of youth, in its desire to break free from the mental bondage and religious superstitions that hold them. As the youth will get more and more saturated with the psychology of revolution, it will come to have a clearer realisation of national bondage and a growing, intense, unquenchable thirst for freedom. It will grow, this feeling of bondage, this insatiable desire for freedom, till, in their righteous anger, the infuriated youth will begin to kill the oppressors. Thus has terrorism been born in the country. It is a phase, a necessary, an inevitable phase of the revolution. Terrorism is not the complete revolution and the revolution is not complete without terrorism. This thesis can be supported by an analysis of any and every revolution in history. Terrorism instils fear in the hearts of the oppressors, it brings hopes of revenge and redemption to the oppressed masses, it gives courage and self-confidence to the wavering, it shatters the spell of the superiority of the ruling class and raises the status of the subject race in the eyes of the world, because it is the most convincing proof of a nation's hunger for freedom. Here in India, as in other countries in the past, terrorism will develop into the revolution and the revolution into independence, social, political and economic.

REVOLUTIONARY METHODS

THIS THEN is what the revolutionaries believe in, that is what they hope to accomplish for their country. They are doing it both openly and secretly, and in their own way. The experience of a century long and world-wide struggle, between the masses and the governing class, is their guide to their goal, and the methods they are following have never been known to have failed.

THE CONGRESS AND THE REVOLUTIONARIES

MEANWHILE, WHAT has the Congress being doing? It has changed its creed from Swaraj to Complete Independence. As a logical sequence to this, one would expect it to declare a war on the British government. Instead, we find, it has declared war against the revolutionaries. The first offensive of the Congress came in the form of a resolution deploring the attempt made on the 23 December,1929, to blow up the Viceroy's Special. It was drafted by Gandhi and he fought tooth and nail for it, with the result that was passed by a trifling majority of 81 in a house of 1,713. Was even this bare majority a result of honest political convictions? Let us quote the opinion of Sarla Devi Chaudharani who has been a devotee of the Congress all her life, in reply. She says: "I discovered in the course of my conversations with a good many of the Mahatma's followers that it was only their sense of personal loyalty to him that was keeping them back from an expression of the independent views and preventing them from voting against any resolution whatsoever that was fathered by Mahatmaji." As to Gandhi's arguments in favour of his proposition, we will deal with them later, when we discuss his article The Cult of the Bomb which is more or less an amplification of his speech in the Congress. There is one fact about this deplorable resolution which we must not lose sight of, and that is this. In spite of the fact, that the Congress is pledged to non-violence and has been actively engaged in carrying on propaganda in its favour for the last ten years, and in spite of the fact also that the supporters of the resolution indulged in abuse, called the revolutionaries 'cowards' and described their actions as 'dastardly'—and one of them even threateningly remarked that if they wanted to be led by Gandhi, they should pass this resolution without any opposition—in spite of all this, the resolution could only be adopted by a dangerously narrow majority. That demonstrates, beyond the shadow of a doubt, how solidly the country is backing the revolutionaries. In a way Gandhi deserved our thanks for having brought the question up for discussion and thus having shown to the world at large that even the Congress— that stronghold of non-violence—is at least as much, if not more, with the revolutionaries as with him.

GANDHI ON WAR PATH

HAVING ACHIEVED a victory which cost him more than a defeat, Gandhi has returned to the attack in his article The Cult of the Bomb. We will give it our closest attention before proceeding further. That article consists of three things—his faith, his opinion and his arguments. We will not discuss what is a matter of faith with him because reason has little in common with faith. Let us then take such of his opinion as are backed by arguments and his arguments proper, against what he calls violence and discuss them one by one.

DO THE MASSES BELIEVE IN NON-VIOLENCE

HE THINKS that on the basis of his experience during his latest tour in the country, he is right in believing that the large masses of Indian humanity are yet untouched by the spirit of violence and that non-violence has come to stay as a political weapon. Let him not delude himself on the experiences of his latest tour in the country. Though it is true that the average leader confines his tours to places where only the mail train can conveniently land him while Gandhi has extended his tour limit to where a motorcar can take him, the practice of staying only with the richest people in the places visited, of spending most of his time on being complimented by his devotees in private and public, and of granting Darshan now and then to the illiterate masses whom he claims to understand so well, disqualifies him from claiming to know the mind of the masses. No man can claim to know a people's mind by seeing them from the public platform and giving them Darshan and Updesh. He can at the most claim to have told the masses what he thinks about things. Has Gandhi, during recent years, mixed in the social life of the masses? Has he sat with the peasant round the evening fire and tried to know what he thinks? Has he passed a single evening in the company of a factory labourer and shared with him his vowes? (sic). We have, and therefore we claim to know what the masses think. We assure Gandhi that the average Indian, like the average human being, understands little of the fine theological niceties about *Ahimsa* and loving one's enemy. The way of the world is like this. You have a friend: you love him, sometimes so much that you even die for him. You have an enemy: you shun him, you fight against him and, if possible, kill him. The gospel of the revolutionaries is simple and straight. It is what has been since the days of Adam and Eve, and no man has any difficulty about understanding it. We affirm that the masses of India are solidly with us because we know it from personal experience. The day is not far off when they will flock in their thousands to work the will of the Revolution.

THE GOSPEL OF LOVE

GANDHI DECLARES that his faith in the efficacy of non-violence has increased. That is to say, he believes more and more, that through his gospel of love and self-imposed suffering, he hopes someday to convert the foreign rulers to his way of thinking. Now, he has devoted his whole life to the preaching of his wonderful gospel and has practised it with unwavering constance,(sic) as few others have done. Will he let the world know how many enemies of India he has been able to turn into friends? How many O'Dwyers, Readings and Irwins has he been able to convert into friends of India? If none, how can India be expected to share his 'growing faith' that he will be able to persuade or compel England to agree to Indian Independence through the practice of non-violence?

WHAT WOULD HAVE HAPPENED

IF THE bomb, that burst under the Viceroy's Special, had exploded properly, one of the two things suggested by Gandhi would have surely happened. The Viceroy would have either been badly injured or killed. Under such circumstances there certainly would have been no meeting between the leaders of political parties and the Viceroy. The uncalled for and undignified attempt on the part of these individuals, to lower the national prestige by knocking at the gates of the government house with the beggar's bowl in their hands and dominion status on their lips, in spite of the clear terms of the Calcutta Ultimatum, would have been checkmated and the nation would have been the better off for that. If, fortunately, the explosion had been powerful enough to kill the Viceroy, one more enemy of India would have met a well deserved doom. The author of the Meerut prosecutions and the Lahore and Bhusawal persecutions can appear a friend of India only to the enemies of her freedom. In spite of Gandhi and Nehru and their claims to political sagacity and statesmanship, Irwin has succeeded in shattering the unity between different political parties in the country, that had resulted from the boycott of the Simon Commission. Even the Congress today is a house divided against itself. Who else, except the Viceroy and his olive tongue, have we to thank for our grave misfortunes? And yet, there exist people in our country who proclaim him a Friend of India.

THE FUTURE OF THE CONGRESS

THERE MIGHT be those who have no regard for the Congress and hope nothing from it. If Gandhi thinks that the revolutionaries belong to the category, he wrongs them grievously. They fully realise the part played by the Congress in awakening among the ignorant masses a keen desire for freedom. They expect great things of it in the future. Though they hold firmly to their opinion, that so long as persons like Sen Gupta whose wonderful intelligence compels him to discern the hand of the CID in the late attempt to blow up the Viceroy's Special, and persons like Ansari, who think abuse the better part of argument and know so little of politics as to make the ridiculous and fallacious assertion that no nation had achieved freedom by the bomb, have a determining voice in the affairs of the Congress, the country can hope little from it; they are hopefully looking forward to the day, when the mania of non-violence would have passed away from the Congress, and it would march arm in arm with the revolutionaries to their common goal of complete Independence. This year, it has accepted the ideal which the revolutionaries have preached and lived up to more than a quarter of a century. Let us hope the next year will see it endorse their methods also.

VIOLENCE AND MILITARY EXPENDITURE

GANDHI IS OF opinion that as violence has been practised in the country, it has resulted in an increase of military expenditure. If his reference is to revolutionary activities during the last twenty-five years we dispute the accuracy of his statement and challenge him to prove his statement with facts and figures. If, on the other hand, he had the wars that have taken place in India since the British came here in mind, our reply is that even his modest experiment in Ahimsa and Satyagraha which had little to compare in it with the wars for independence produced its effect on the finances of the bureaucracy. Mass action, whether violent or non-violent, whether successful or unsuccessful, is bound to produce the same kind of repercussion on the finances of a state.

THE REFORMS

WHY SHOULD Gandhi mix up the revolutionaries with the various constitutional reforms granted by the government? They never cared or worked for the Morely-Minto Reforms, Montagu Reforms and the like. These the British government threw before the constitutionalist agitators to lure them away from the right path. This was the bribe paid to them for their support to the government in its policy of crushing and uprooting the revolutionaries. These toys—as Gandhi calls them—were sent to India for the benefit of those, who, from time to time, raised the cry of 'Home Rule', 'Self-Government', 'Responsible', 'Full Responsible Government', 'Dominion Status' and such other constitutional names for slavery. The revolutionaries never claim the Reforms as their achievements. They raised the standard of independence long ago. They have lived for it. They have ungrudgingly laid their lives down for the sake of this ideal. They claim that their sacrifices have produced a tremendous change in the mentality of the people. That their efforts have advanced the country a long way on the road to independence, is granted by even those who do not see eye to eye with them in politics.

THE WAY OF PROGRESS

AS TO Gandhi's contention that violence impedes the march of progress and thus directly postpones the day of freedom, we can refer him to so many contemporary instances where violence has led to the social progress and political freedom of the people who practised it. Take the case of Russia and Turkey for example. In both countries the party for progress took over the state orgnisation through an armed revolution. Yet social progress and political freedom have not been impeded. Legislation, backed by force, has made the masses go 'double march' on the road of progress. The solitary example of Afghanistan cannot establish a political formula. It is rather the exception that proves the rule.

FAILURE OF NON-COOPERATION

GANDHI IS of opinion that the great awakening in the people, during the days of non-cooperation, was a result of the preaching of non-violence. It is wrong to assign to non-violence the widespread awakening of the masses which, in fact, is manifested wherever a programme of direct action is adopted. In Russia, for instance, there came about widespread awakening in the peasants and workers when the communists launched forth their great programme of Militant Mass Action, though nobody preached non-violence to them. We will even go further and state that it was mainly the mania for non-violence and Gandhi's compromise mentality that brought about the disruption of the forces that had come together at the call of Mass Action. It is claimed that non-violence can be used as a weapon for righting political wrongs. To say the least, it is a novel idea, yet untried. It failed to achieve what were considered to be the just rights of Indians in South Africa. It failed to bring 'Swaraj within a year' to the Indian masses in spite of the untiring labours of an army of national workers and one and a quarter crores of rupees. More recently, it failed to win for the Bardoli peasants what the leaders of the Satyagraha movement had promised them—the famous irreducible minimum of Gandhi and Patel. We know of no other trials non-violence has had on a country-wide scale. Up to this time non-violence has been blessed with one result—Failure. Little wonder, then, that the country refuses to give it another trial. In fact Satyagraha as preached by Gandhi is a form of agitation—a protest, leading up invariably, as has already been seen, to a compromise. It can hardly be of any use to a nation striving for national independence which can never come as the result of a compromise. The sooner we recognise that there can be no compromise between independence and slavery, the better.

IS IT A NEW ERA

'WE ARE entering upon a new era', thinks Gandhi. The mere act of defining Swaraj as Complete Independence, this technical change in the Congress constitution, can hardly constitute a new era. It will be a great day indeed when the Congress will decide upon a country-wide programme of Mass Action, based on well recognised revolutionary principles. Till then the unfurling of the flag of Independence is a mockery and we concur with the following remarks of Sarla Devi Chaudharani which she recently made in a press interview.

"The unfurling of the Flag of Independence", she says, "at just one minute after midnight of the 31 December, 1929, was too stagy for words- just as the GOC and the assistant GOC and others in gaudy uniforms were card board Grand Officers Commanding.

"The fact that the unfurling of the flag of Independence lay hanging in the balance till midnight of that date, and that the scales might have been turned at even the eleventh hour fiftyninth minute had a message from the Viceroy or the Secretary of State come to the Congress granting Dominion Status, proves that Independence is not a heart hunger (sic) of the leaders but that the declaration of it is only like a petulant child's retort. It would have been a worthy action of the Indian National Congress if Independence was achieved first and declared afterwards." It is true that the Congress orators will henceforth harangue the masses on Complete Independence instead of Dominion Status. They will call upon the people to prepare for a struggle in which one party is to deliver blows and the other is simply to receive them, till beaten and demoralised beyond hope of recovery. Can such a thing be named a struggle and can it ever lead the country to Complete Independence? It is all very well to hold fast to the highest ideal worthy of a nation, but it is nonetheless necessary to adopt the best, the most efficacious and tried means to achieve it, are you became the laughing stock of the whole world.

NO BULLYING PLEASE

GANDHI HAS called upon all those who are not past reason to withdraw their support from the revolutionaries and condemn their actions so that "our deluded patriots may, for want of nourishment to their violent spirit, realise the futility of violence and the great harm that violent activities have every time done". How easy and convenient it is to call people deluded, to declare them to be past reason, to call upon the public to withdraw its support and condemn them so that they may get isolated and be forced to suspend their activities, specially when a man holds the confidence of an influential section of the public. It is a pity that Gandhi does not and will not understand revolutionary psychology in spite of the life-long experience of public life. Life is a precious thing. It is clear to everyone. If a man becomes a revolutionary, if he goes about with his life in the hollow of his hand ready to sacrifice it at any moment, he does not do so merely for the fun of it. He does not risk his life merely because sometimes, when the crowd is in a sympathetic mood, it cries 'Bravo' in appreciation. He does it because his reason forces him to take that course, because his conscience dictates it. A revolutionary believes in reason more than anything. It is to reason, and reason alone, that he bows. No amount of abuse and condemnation, even if it emanates from the highest of the high can turn him from his set purpose. To think that a revolutionary will give up his ideas if public support and appreciation is withdrawn from him, is the highest folly. Many a revolutionary has, ere now, stepped on the scaffold and laid his life down for the cause, regardless of the curses that the constitutionalist agitators rained plentifully upon him. If you will have the revolutionaries suspend their activities, reason with them squarely. That is the one and the only way. For the rest let there be no doubt in anybody's mind. A revolutionary is the last person on earth to submit to bullying.

AN APPEAL

WE TAKE this opportunity to appeal to our countrymen—to the youth, to the workers and peasants, to the revolutionary intelligentsia—to come forward and join us in carrying aloft the banner of freedom. Let us establish a new order of society in which political and economic exploitation will be an impossibility. In the name of those gallant men and women who willingly accepted death so that we, their descendants, may lead a happier life, who toiled ceaselessly and perished for the poor, the famished, and exploited millions of India, we call upon every patriot to take up the fight in all seriousness. Let nobody toy with the nation's freedom which is her very life, by making psychological experiments in non-violence and such other novelties. Our slavery is our shame. When shall we have courage and wisdom enough to be able to shake ourselves free of it? What is our great heritage of civilisation and culture worth if we have not enough self-respect left in us to prevent us from bowing surveillance to the commands of foreigners and paying homage to their flag and kind?

VICTORY OR DEATH

THERE IS no crime that Britain has not committed in India. Deliberate misrule has reduced us to paupers, has 'bled us white'. As a race and a people we stand dishonoured and outraged. Do people still expect us to forget and to forgive? We shall have our revenge—a people's righteous revenge on the tyrant. Let cowards fall back and cringe for compromise and peace. We ask not for mercy and we give no quarter. Ours is a war to the end—to Victory or Death.

LONG LIVE REVOLUTION

President,
Hindustan Socialist Republican Association.

Annexure-IV

To the Young Political Workers

Dear Comrades,

Our movement is passing through a very important phase at present. After a year's fierce struggle, some definite proposals regarding the constitutional reforms have been formulated by the Round Table Conference and the Congress leaders have been invited to give this ...* think it desirable in the present circumstances to call off their movement. Whether they decide in favour or against is a matter of little importance to us. The present movement is bound to end in some sort of compromise. The compromise may be effected sooner or later. And compromise is not such ignoble and deplorable a thing as we generally think. It is rather an indispensable factor in the political strategy. Any nation that rose against the oppressors was bound to fail in the beginning, and to gain partial reforms during the medieval period of its struggle through compromises. And it is only at the last stage–having fully organised all the forces and resources of the nation–that it could possibly strike the final blow in which it might succeed to shatter the ruler's government. But even then it might fail, which made some sort of compromise inevitable. Bhagat Singh illustrated his point by the Russian example. In 1905 a revolutionary movement broke out in Russia. All the leaders were very hopeful. Lenin had returned from the foreign countries where he had taken refuge. He was conducting the struggle. People came to tell him that a dozen landlords were killed and a score of their mansions were burnt. Lenin responded by telling them to return and to kill twelve hundred landlords and burn as many of their palaces. In his opinion that would have meant something if revolution failed. Duma (parliament) was introduced. The same Lenin advocated the

*some words are missing here.'

view of participating in the Duma. This was what happened in 1907. In 1906 he was opposed to the participation in the second one whose rights had been curtailed. Reaction was gaining the upper hand and Lenin wanted to use the floor of the Duma as a platform to discuss socialist ideas.

After the 1917 revolution, when the Bolsheviks were forced to sign the Brest Litovsk Treaty, everyone except Lenin was opposed to it. But Lenin said: `Peace'. "Peace and again peace: peace at any cost—even at the cost of many of the Russian provinces to be yielded to German War Lord". When some anti-Bolshevik people condemned Lemin for this treaty, he declared frankly that the Bolsheviks were not in a position to face the German onslaught and they preferred the treaty to the complete annihilation of the Bolshevik government.

The thing that I wanted to point out was that compromise is an essential weapon which has to be wielded every now and then as the struggle develops. But the thing that we must keep always before us is the idea of the movement. We must always maintain a clear notion as to the aim for the achievement of which we are fighting. That helps us to verify the success and failures of our movements and we can easily formulate the future programme. Tilak's policy, quite apart from the ideal, i.e. his strategy, was the best. You are fighting to get sixteen annas from your enemy, you get only one anna. Pocket it and fight for the rest. What we note in the moderates is of their ideal. They start to achieve one anna and they can't get it. The revolutionaries must always keep in mind that they are striving for a complete revolution. Complete mastery of power in their hands. Compromises are dreaded because the conservatives try to disband the revolutionary forces after the compromise. But able and bold revolutionary leaders can save the movement from such pitfalls. We must be very careful at such junctures to avoid any sort of confusion of the real issues, especially the goal. The British Labour leaders betrayed their real struggle and have been reduced to mere hypocrite imperialists. In my opinion the diehard conservatives are better to us than these polished imperialist Labour leaders. About the tactics and strategy one should study the life-work of Lenin. His definite views on the subject of compromise will be found in "Left Wing" Communism.

I have said that the present movement, i.e. the present struggle, is bound to end in some sort of compromise or complete failure.

I said that, because in my opinion, this time the real revolutionary forces have not been invited into the arena. This is a struggle dependent upon the middle class, shopkeepers and a few capitalists. Both these, and particularly the latter, can never dare to risk its property or possessions in any struggle. The real revolutionary armies are in the villages and in factories, the peasantry and the labourers. But our bourgeois leaders do not and cannot dare to tackle them. The sleeping lion once awakened from its slumber shall become irresistible even after the achievement of what our leaders aim at. After his first experience with the Ahmedabad labourers in 1920 Mahatma Gandhi declared: "We must not tamper with the labourers. It is dangerous to make political use of the factory proletariat" (The Times, May 1921). Since then, they never dared to approach them. There remains the peasantry. The Bardoli resolution of 1922 clearly defines the horror the leaders felt when they saw the gigantic peasant class rising to shake off not only the domination of an alienation but also the yoke of the landlords.

It is there that our leaders prefer a surrender to the British than to the peasantry. Leave alone Pt. Jawahar Lal. Can you point out any leader who made any effort to organise the peasants or the labourers? No, they will not run the risk. There they lack. That is why I say they never meant a complete revolution. Through economic and administrative pressure they hoped to get a few more reforms, a few more concessions for the Indian capitalists. That is why I say that this movement is doomed to die, may be after some sort of compromise or even without. The young workers who in all sincerity raise the cry `Long Live Revolution,' are not well organised and strong enough to carry the movement themselves. As a matter of fact, even our great leaders, with the exception of perhaps Pt. Motilal Nehru, do not dare to take any responsibility on their shoulders, that is why every now and then they surrender unconditionally before Gandhi. In spite of their differences, they never oppose him seriously and the resolution have to be carried for the Mahatma.

In these circumstances, let me warn the sincere young workers who seriously mean a revolution, that harder times are coming. Let them beware lest they should get confused or disheartened. After the experience made through two struggles of the Great Gandhi, we are in a better position to form a clear idea of our present position and the future programme.

Allow me to state the case in the simplest manner. You cry, `Long Live Revolution.' Let me assume that you really mean it. According to our definition of the term, as stated in our statement in the Assembly Bomb Case, revolution means the complete overthrow of the existing social order and its replacement with the socialist order. For that purpose our immediate aim is the achievement of power. As a matter of fact, the state, the government machinery is just a weapon in the hands of the ruling class to further and safeguard its interest. We want to snatch and handle it to utilise it for the consummation of our ideal, i.e., the social reconstruction on new, i.e. Marxist basis. For this purpose we are fighting to handle . the government machinery. All along we have to educate the masses and to create a favourable atmosphere for our social programme. In the struggles we can best train and educate them.

With these things clear before us, i.e. our immediate and ultimate object having been clearly put, we can now proceed with the examination of the present situation. We must always be very candid and quite business-like while analyzing any situation.

We know that since a hue and cry was raised about the Indian's participation in and share in the responsibility of the Indian government, the Minto-Morley Reforms were introduced, which formed the Viceroy's council with consultation rights only. During the Great War, when the Indian help was needed the most, promises about self-government were made and the existing reforms were introduced. Limited legislative powers have been entrusted to the Assembly but subject to the goodwill of the Viceroy. Now is the third stage.

Now reforms are being discussed and are to be introduced in the near future. How can our young men judge them? This is a question; I do not know by what standard are the Congress leaders going to judge them. But for us, the revolutionaries, we can have the following criteria:

1. Extent of responsibility transferred to the shoulders of the Indians.
2. Form of the Government institutions that are going to be introduced and the extent of the right of participation given to the masses.
3. Future prospects and the safeguards.

These might require a little further elucidation. In the first place, we can easily judge the extent of responsibility given to our people by the control our representatives will have on the executive. Up till now, the executive was never made responsible to the Legislative Assembly and the Viceroy had the veto power, which rendered all the efforts of the elected members futile. Thanks to the efforts of the Swaraj Party, the Viceroy was forced every now and then to use these extraordinary powers to shamelessly trample the solemn decisions of the national representatives under foot. It is already too well known to need further discussion.

Now in the first place we must see the method of the executive formation: Whether the executive is to be elected by the members of a popular assembly or is to be imposed from above as before, and further, whether it shall be responsible to the house or shall absolutely affront it as in the past?

As regards the second item, we can judge it through the scope of franchise. The property qualifications making a man eligible to vote should be altogether abolished and universal suffrage be introduced instead. Every adult, both male and female, should have the right to vote. At present we can simply see how far the franchise has been extended.

As for the form, we have the bicameral government. In my opinion the upper house is much a bourgeois superstition or trap. According to me unicameral government is the only best we can expect.

I may here make a mention about provincial autonomy. But from whatever I have heard, I can only say that the Governor imposed from above, equipped with extraordinary powers, higher and above the legislative, shall prove to be no less than a despot. Let us better call it the 'provincial tyranny' instead of 'autonomy'. This is a strange type of democratisation of the state institution.

The third item is quite clear. During the last two years the British politicians have been trying to undo Montague's promise for another dole of reforms to be bestowed every ten years till the British Treasury exhausts.

We can see what they have decided about the future.

Let me make it clear that we do not analyse these things to rejoice over the achievement, but to form a clear idea about our situation, so that we may enlighten the masses and prepare them for further struggle. For us, compromise never means surrender, but a step forward and some rest. That is all and nothing else.

HAVING DISCUSSED the present situation, let us proceed to discuss the future programme and the line of action we ought to adopt.

As I have already stated, for any revolutionary party, a definite programme is very essential. For, you must know that revolution means action. It means a change brought about deliberately by an organised and systematic work, as opposed to sudden and unorganised or spontaneous change or breakdown. And for the formulation of a programme, one must necessarily study:

1. The goal,

2. The premises from where we are to start, i.e. the existing conditions;

3. The course of action, i.e. means and methods.

Unless one has a clear notion about these three factors, one cannot discuss anything about programme.

We have discussed at present situation to some extent. The goal has been slightly touched. We want a socialist revolution, the indispensable preliminary to which is the political revolution. That is what we want. The political revolution does not mean the transfer of state for more crudely, the power, from the hands of the British to the Indians, but to those Indians who are at one with us as to the final goal, or to the more precise, the power to be transferred to the revolutionary party through popular support. After that, to proceed in right earnest is to organise the reconstruction of the whole society on the socialist basis. If you do not mean this revolution, then please have mercy. Stop shouting, `Long Live Revolution.' The term revolution is too sacred, at least to us, to be so lightly used or misused. But if you say you are for the national revolution and the aims of your struggle is an Indian republic of the type of the United States of America, then I ask you to please let me know on what forces you rely that will help you bring about that revolution. The only forces on which you can rely to bring about any revolution, whether national or the socialist, are the peasantry and the labour. Congress leaders do not dare to organise those forces. You have seen it in this movement. They know it better than anybody else that without these forces they are absolutely helpless. When they passed the resolution of complete independence—that really meant a revolution—they did not mean it. They had to do it under pressure of the younger element, and then they wanted to use it as a threat to achieve their hearts' desire—Dominion Status. You can easily judge it by studying the resolutions of the last three sessions of the Congress. I mean Madras, Calcutta and Lahore. At Calcutta, they passed a resolution asking for Dominion Status within twelve months, otherwise they would be forced to adopt complete independence as their object, and in all solemnity waited for some such gift till midnight after the 31st December, 1929. Then they found themselves "honour bound" to adopt the Independence resolution, otherwise they did not mean it. But even then Mahatmaji made no secret of the fact that the door (for compromise) was open. That was the real spirit. At the very outset they knew that their movement could not but end in some compromise. It is this half-heartedness that we hate, not the compromise at a particular stage in the struggle. Anyway, we were discussing the forces on which you can depend for a revolution. But if you say that you will approach the peasants and labourers to enlist their active support, let me tell you that they are not going to be fooled by any sentimental talk. They ask you quite candidly: what are they going to gain by your revolution for which you demand· their sacrifices, what difference does it make to them whether Lord Reading is the head of the Indian government or Sir Purshotamdas Thakordas? What difference for a peasant if Sir Tej Bahadur Sapru replaces Lord Irwin? It is useless to appeal to his national sentiment. You can't `use' him for your purpose; you shall have to mean seriously and to make him understand that the revolution is going to be his and for his good. The revolution of the proletariat and for the proletariat.

When you have formulated this clear-cut idea about your goals, you can proceed in right earnest to organise your forces for such an action. Now there are two different phases through which you shall have to pass. First, the preparation; second, the action.

After the present movement ends you will find disgust and some disappointment amongst the sincere revolutionary workers. But you need not worry. Leave sentimentalism aside. Be prepared to face the facts. Revolution is a very difficult task. It is beyond the power of any man to make a revolution. Neither can it be brought about on any appointed date. It is brought about by special environments, social and economic. The function of an organised party is to utilise any such opportunity offered by these circumstances. And to prepare the masses and organise the forces for the revolution is a very difficult task. And that requires a very great sacrifice on the part of the revolutionary workers. Let me make it clear that if you are a businessman or an established wordly or family man, please don't play with fire. As a leader you are of no use to the party. We have already very many such leaders who spare some evening hours for delivering speeches. They are useless. We require—to use the term so dear to Lenin—the "professional revolutionaries". The whole-time workers who have no other ambitions or life-work except the revolution. The greater the number of such workers organised into a party, the greater the chances of your success.

To proceed systematically, what you need the most is a party with workers of the type discussed above with clear-cut ideas and keen perception and ability of initiative and quick decisions. The party shall have iron discipline and it need not necessarily be an underground party, rather the contrary. Though the policy of voluntarily going to jail should altogether be abandoned. That will create a number of workers who shall be forced to lead an underground life. They should carry on the work with the same zeal. And it is this group of workers that shall produce worthy leaders for the real opportunity.

. The party requires workers which can be recruited only through the youth movement. Hence we find the youth movement as the starting point of our programme. The youth movement should organise study circles, class lectures and publication of leaflets, pamphlets, books and periodicals. This is the best recruiting and training ground for political workers.

Those young men who may have matured their ideas and may find themselves ready to devote their life to the cause, may be transferred to the party. The party workers shall always guide and control the work of the youth movement as well. The party should start with the work of mass propaganda. It is very essential. One of the fundamental causes of the failure of the Ghadar Party (1914-15) was the ignorance, apathy and sometimes active opposition of the masses. And apart from that, it is essential for gaining the active sympathy of and organising the peasants and workers. The name of party or rather,' a communist party. This party of political workers, bound by strict discipline, should handle all other movements. It shall have to organise the peasants and workers' parties, labour unions, and may even venture to capture the

'obviously a few words are missing here.

Congress and kindred political bodies. And in order to create political consciousness, not only of national politics but class politics as well, the party should organise a big publishing campaign. Subjects on all proletens (;) enlightening the masses of the socialist theory shall be within easy reach and distributed widely. The writings should be simple and clear.

There are certain people in the labour movement who enlist some absurd ideas about the economic liberty of the peasants and workers without political freedom. They are demagogues or muddle-headed people. Such ideas are unimaginable and preposterous. We mean the economic liberty of the masses, and for that very purpose we are striving to win the political power. No doubt in the beginning, we shal have to fight for little economic demands and privileges of these classes. But these struggles are the best means for educating them for a final struggle to conquer political power.

Apart from these, there shall necessarily be organised a military department. This is very important. At times its need is felt very badly. But at that time you cannot start and formulate such a group with substantial means to act effectively. Perhaps this is the topic that needs a careful explanation. There is very great probability of my being misunderstood on this subject. Apparently I have acted like a terrorist. But I am not a terrorist. I am a revolutionary who has got such definite ideas of a lengthy programme as is being discussed here. My "comrades in arms" might accuse me, like Ram Prasad Bismil, for having been subjected to certain sort of reaction in the condemned cell, which is not true. I have got the same ideas, same convictions, same zeal and same spirit as I used to have outside, perhaps—nay, decidedly—better. Hence I warn my readers to be careful while reading my words. They should not try to read anything between the lines. Let me announce with all the strength at my command that I am not a terrorist and I never was, except perhaps in the beginning of my revolutionary career. And I am convinced that we cannot gain anything through those methods. One can easily judge it from the history of the Hindustan Socialist Republican Association. All our activities were directed towards an aim, i.e. identifying ourselves with the great movement as its military wing. If anybody has misunderstood me, let him amend his ideas. I do not mean that bombs and pistols are useless, rather the contrary. But if mean to say that mere bomb-throwing is not only useless but sometimes harmful. The military department of the party should always keep ready all the war-material it can command for any emergency. It should back the political work of the party. It cannot and should not work independently.

On these lines indicated above, the party should proceed with its work. Through periodical meetings and conferences they should go on educating and enlightening their workers on all topics.

If you start the work on these lines, you shall have to be very sober. The programme requires at least twenty years for its fulfilment. Cast aside the youthful dreams of a revolution within ten years of Gandhi's utopian promises of Swaraj in One Year. It requires neither the emotion nor the death, but the life of constant struggle, suffering and sacrifice. Crush your individuality first. Shake off the dreams of personal comfort. Then start to work. Inch by inch you shall have to proceed. It needs courage, perseverance and very strong determination. No difficulties and no hardships shall discourage you. No failure and betrayals shall dishearten you. No travails (!) imposed upon you shall snuff out the revolutionary will in you. Through the ordeal of sufferings and sacrifice you shall come out victorious. And these individual victories shall be the valuable assets of the revolution.

LONG LIVE REVOLUTION

2nd February, 1931.

Bibliography

AJOY GHOSH
Bhagat Singh and his Comrades

A.S. BARDHAN
Bhagat Singh: Pages from the Life of Martyr

BIPAN CHANDRA
Nationalism and Colonialism in Modern India

BIPAN CHANDRA
India's Struggle or Independence

CHARLES FREER ANDREWS
India and the Simon Report

Collected Works of Mahatma Gandhi, Vol. XIV

DAVID M. LAUSHEY
Bengal Terrorism and Marxist Left

GURDEV SINGH DEOL
Shaheed Bhagat Singh

GURDEV SINGH DEOL
Sardar Bhagat Singh

HANSRAJ RAHBAR
Bhagat Singh and His Thought

I. MALLIKARJUNA SHARMA
Role of Revolutionaries in the Indian Freedom Struggle

JATINDRANATH SANYAL
Sardar Bhagat Singh

J.C. CHATTERJEE
Indian Revolutionaries in Conference

J.N. VAJPEYI
The Extremist Movement in India

KALICHARAN GHOSH
Roll of Honour

KAUSHLYA DEVI DUBLISH
Revolutionaries and their Activities

K.K. KHULLAR
Shaheed Bhagat Singh

MANMATHNATH GUPTA
Bhagat Singh and His Times

MANMATHNATH GUPTA
History of the Indian Revolutionary Movement

SACHINDRANATH SANYAL
Sardar Bhagat Singh

SACHINDRANATH SANYAL
Bandi Jibon

SHAIESHWAR NATH
Terrorism in India

SHIV VERMA
Selected writtings of Shaheed Bhagat Singh

S.R. BAKSHI
Bhagat Singh and His Ideology

SUMIT SARKAR
Modern India

VIRENDRA SANDHU (EDITED)
Bhagat Singh Letter and Documents

VISHWANATH VAISHAMPAYAN
Chandrasekhar Azad, Vol. I, II, III

Index